The Cato Institute

The Cato Institute is named for the libertarian pamphlets *Cato's Letters,* which were inspired by the Roman Stoic Cato the Younger. Written by John Trenchard and Thomas Gordon, *Cato's Letters* were widely read in the American colonies in the early eighteenth century and played a major role in laying the philosophical foundation for the revolution that followed.

The erosion of civil and economic liberties in the modern world has occurred in concert with a widening array of social problems. These disturbing developments have resulted from a major failure to examine social problems in terms of the fundamental principles of human dignity, economic welfare, and justice.

The Cato Institute aims to broaden public policy debate by sponsoring programs designed to assist both the scholar and the concerned layperson in analyzing questions of political economy.

The programs of the Cato Institute include the sponsorship and publication of basic research in social philosophy and public policy; publication of major journals on the scholarship of liberty and commentary on political affairs; production of debate forums for radio; and organization of an extensive program of symposia, seminars, and conferences.

CATO INSTITUTE
747 Front Street
San Francisco, California 94111

The Great Depression
—— and ——
New Deal Monetary Policy

The Great Depression
—— and ——
New Deal Monetary Policy

Garet Garrett
and
Murray N. Rothbard

With a Foreword by Robert L. Formaini

CATO PAPER No. 13

CATO INSTITUTE
San Francisco, California

The essay by Garet Garrett is reprinted from *A Bubble That Broke the World* (Boston: Little, Brown, and Company, 1932).

"The New Deal and the International Monetary System" by Murray N. Rothbard originally appeared in *Watershed of Empire: Essays on New Deal Foreign Policy,* Leonard P. Liggio and James J. Martin, eds. (Colorado Springs: Ralph Myles, 1976) and is reprinted with permission of Ralph Myles, Publisher.

Library of Congress Cataloging in Publication Data

Garrett, Garet, 1878–1954.
    The Great Depression and New Deal monetary policy.

    (Cato paper ; 13)
    Bibliography: p.
    1. Depressions — 1929 — History — Addresses, essays, lectures. 2. Monetary policy — United States — History — Addresses, essays, lectures. 3. Finance — United States — History — Addresses, essays, lectures. I. Rothbard, Murray Newton, 1926– joint author. II. Title.
HB3717 1929.G37 1980   338.5′42   80-36791
ISBN 0-932790-19-4

Printed in the United States of America.

CATO INSTITUTE
747 Front Street
San Francisco, California 94111

CONTENTS

51489

FOREWORD

The lack of the fabulous may make my work dull. But I shall be
satisfied if it be thought useful by those who wish to know the exact character of events now past, which, human nature being what
it is, will recur in similar or analogous forms.

Thucydides
The Peloponnesian Wars

Putting two essays by such admittedly disparate authors as Murray Rothbard and Garet Garrett together in the same volume may
strike students of economic history as a bit bizarre. After all, can
a modern anarchist and a seemingly ancient, solemn, and stalwart
defender of the American republic and Constitution have similar
things to say about such momentous events as the First World
War and the Great Depression?

Those acquainted with these authors will be less surprised than
the uninitiated. But who today remembers Garet Garrett at all?
Indeed, who even considers the First World War relevant to our
present economic condition? And as for Rothbard, what does a
libertarian anarchist have in common with an intellectual pillar of
the Old Right? The answer is: plenty.

The tapestry of history is woven from strands of continuous
time, which is to say that all historical demarcations are arbitrary.
One can, as a matter of convenience, take the year 1914 or 1945 as
a "starting point" from which to investigate succeeding events,
but the best chronicles of history are written by men who understand that time is a continuum and indivisible. It is probably for
this reason that Thucydides was able to predict that his history
would prove significant to future generations since events would
repeat themselves. Consider the present state of our economic affairs; is there any unique factor or set of conditions that a
nineteenth-century economist would not have recognized? Indeed, we might expand the question to include even Adam Smith

and his generation. Inflation, unemployment, public debts, imbalances of trade, tariffs and trade quotas, concentration and monopoly, and a lengthy checklist of other symptoms, causes, and effects of modern policy were known and examined even in the eighteenth century; they have been analyzed and debated throughout the history of the world. For all that, we face today the unhappy possibility of hyperinflation, war, and depression.

Both Garrett and Rothbard saw that the United States, ignoring the accumulated wisdom of centuries, took a fateful turn for the worse in the years prior to the first great war. The American nation, the undisputed world power after the Spanish-American War, was seized with a frenzy of internationalism, a philosophy endorsed and articulated by the nation's president, Woodrow Wilson. With the election of Wilson, the Eastern combination of intellectuals and certain large banking interests had a president able and willing to ally American and European economic interests. At last the dormant power of the American productive apparatus could be harnessed for interventionism abroad on a scale never before seen in history. It is no accident that the country in those years adopted the progressive income tax and the Federal Reserve System. Without these two fundamental changes in American finance, it is unlikely that any president could have embarked upon the interventionist course Wilson plotted for America.

Wars, and the system of alliances that precede them, require money. In ancient times, a major constraint on combatants was the extremely high cost of war. The entry of the United States into the First World War signaled not only a gigantic infusion of arms, men, and materials, but more importantly, from the standpoint of both the domestic economy and our belligerent allies, an injection of vast sums of money, extended by America on "credit." Vast transfers of wealth from Americans to peoples and governments all over the world took place. These "loans" were, for the most part, repudiated. But a nation that has suddenly discovered the power of the "state" need not fear such eventualities! Were we not very, very wealthy?

Looking back at the assurances of politicians during this era is, of course, amusing; their statements and errors seem incredible to us. They were, after all, advised by the most noted economists of their era. Unfortunately, we today are no less seduced by the same arguments. Why have we learned so little? Are we not still taxing our own citizens to "defend" the citizens of other countries, countries whose products, thus subsidized by us, we must restrict by import quotas and excise taxes?

Are we not still inflating the currency and living on credit, on borrowed time? Has the power of the mass delusion, the urge to "spend one's way to prosperity," afflicted the modern American electorate less than it afflicted our grandfathers? In short, has Garrett's "cosmology of the bubble" appreciably altered over time? To ask is to answer.

World War I was a watershed in American history. The cartelization of American industry, begun during the Progressive Era, came to fruition. Internationalism swept everything before it in a hysterical crusade to democratize the world. The cult of American nationalism was born. From this base, the New Freedom of Wilson grew toward the New Deal of Roosevelt, creating the modern American welfare-warfare state. Interventionism abroad required interventionism at home; government meddling in the affairs of other nations lay the groundwork for its meddling in the affairs of every American. Yet only one citizen in a hundred had any understanding of how closely these events were related, or why one followed the other necessarily and predictably.

Garrett began by playing Cato to Roosevelt's Caesar (*The Revolution Was*) and ended as an American Tacitus (*Rise of Empire*), withdrawn from a civilization he could no longer support, feeling, as his Roman counterpart long ago must have felt, that the end was surely near.

Contrast with Garrett's experience that of Murray Rothbard. Beginning his analysis of New Deal monetary policy where Garrett leaves off, he is unencumbered by any direct memories of a time when "things were better." What he knows of the free market, and political freedom as well, comes from abstract economic analysis and the history of earlier periods. Garrett and Rothbard both wrote histories of America, but what different histories they are! For Garrett, *The American Story* begins with the revolution, where refugees from absolutist, collectivist Europe throw off their old ideas and, with them, their chains. The story comes full circle and ends with the New Deal and the cold war advance to empire. It is Rome all over again.

Rothbard finds a different America, one *Conceived in Liberty*, subverted not so much by European intellectuals as by her own unfortunate counterrevolution—that very constitution Garrett so revered! While Garrett gives the benefit of the doubt to bankers, politicians, and even economists, Rothbard perceives self-serving abuse of privilege and trust. Where Garrett observes presidents being led astray by ill-informed advisers, Rothbard sees perfidy, and the subversion of America's basic anarchic tradition, by a collection of second-rate minds acting in their own interests at the expense of everyone else. Though Garrett went from optimism to pessimism, Rothbard has moved in the opposite direction, becoming more convinced each year that the ultimate triumph of liberty is at hand. Such a development would surely vindicate their lifelong dedication to a single idea, best expressed by the poet Lucan:

> I will follow your name, Liberty, even when it has become only a dream.

Always searching for historical details that support his basic thesis, in the selected essay Rothbard chronicles the early international policy of New Deal bankers and theoreticians. Like Garrett, he is an opponent of inflation; hence, he deplores the moronic maneuvering with gold, the attempted "price level adjustments" backed by Irving Fisher, and the Bretton Woods agreements—all of them manifestations of advantages pursued by a few citizens at the expense of the rest. This essay is one of the least known of Rothbard's works, a situation this reprinting should help rectify.

These essays paint a broad picture of American finance throughout most of this century. Both authors, dedicated opponents of central planning and fiat money, ardent pacifists and noninterventionists, and eloquent advocates of the free market, are, in spite of all their dissimilarities, well coupled in this publication. Garrett's prose has always been distinctive, a joy to read for those like me who agree that serious writing needn't be dry and full of clichés. Rothbard, joyously cynical and irreverent, remains a powerful antipode of all conventional interpretations. Together, they are irresistible.

March, 1980   Robert L. Formaini
                                                    San Francisco, California

From *A Bubble That Broke the World*

Garet Garrett

Cosmology of the Bubble

The Lord giveth increase, but man devised credit.

Mass delusions are not rare. They salt the human story. The hallucinatory types are well known; so also is the sudden variation called mania, generally localized, like the tulip mania in Holland many years ago or the common-stock mania of a recent time in Wall Street. But a delusion affecting the mentality of the entire world at one time was hitherto unknown. All our experience with it is original.

This is a delusion about credit. And whereas from the nature of credit it is to be expected that a certain line will divide the view between creditor and debtor, the irrational fact in this case is that for more than ten years debtors and creditors together have pursued the same deceptions. In many ways, as will appear, the folly of the lender has exceeded the extravagance of the borrower.

The general shape of this universal delusion may be indicated by three of its familiar features.

First, the idea that the panacea for debt is credit.

Debt in the present order of magnitude began with the World War. Without credit, the war could not have continued above four months; with benefit of credit it went more than four years. Victory followed the credit. The price was appalling debt. In Europe the war debt was both internal and external. The American war debt was internal only. This was the one country that borrowed nothing; not only did it borrow nothing, but parallel to its own war exertions it loaned to its European associates more than ten billion dollars. This the European governments owed to the United States Treasury, besides what they owed to one another and to their own people. Europe's attack upon her debt, both internal and external, was a resort to credit. She called upon this country for immense sums of private credit—sums which before the war had been unimaginable—saying that unless American credit provided her with the ways and means to begin moving her burden of debt she would be unable to move it at all.

Result: The burden of Europe's private debt to this country now is greater than the burden of her war debt; and the war debt, with arrears of interest, is greater than it was the day the peace was signed. And it is not Europe alone. Debt was the economic terror of the world when the war ended. How to pay it was the colossal problem. Yet you will find hardly a nation, hardly any subdivision of a nation, state, city, town, or region that has not multiplied its debt since the war. The aggregate of this increase is prodigious, and a very high proportion of it represents recourse to credit to avoid payment of debt.

Second, a social and political doctrine, now widely accepted, beginning with the premise that people are entitled to certain betterments of life. If they cannot immediately afford them, that is, if out of their own resources these betterments cannot be provided, nevertheless people are entitled to them, and credit must provide them. And lest it should sound unreasonable, the conclusion is annexed that if the standard of living be raised by credit, as of course it may be for a while, then people will be better creditors, better customers, better to live with and able at last to pay their debts willingly.

Result: Probably one half of all government, national and civic, in the area of western civilization is either bankrupt or in acute distress from having overborrowed according to this doctrine. It has ruined the credit of countries that had no war debts to begin with, countries that were enormously enriched by the war trade, and countries that were created new out of the war. Now as credit fails and the standards of living tend to fall from the planes on which credit for a while sustained them, there is political dismay. You will hear that government itself is in jeopardy. How shall government avert social chaos, how shall it survive, without benefit of credit? How shall people live as they have learned to live, and as they are entitled to live, without benefit of credit?

Shall they be told to go back? They will not go back. They will rise first. Thus rhetoric, indicating the emotional position. It does not say that what people are threatening to rise against is the payment of debt for credit devoured. When they have been living on credit beyond their means the debt overtakes them. If they tax themselves to pay it, that means going back a little. If they repudiate their debt, that is the end of their credit. In this dilemma the ideal solution, so recommended even to the creditor, is more credit, more debt.

Third, the argument that prosperity is a product of credit, whereas from the beginning of economic thought it had been supposed that prosperity was from the increase and exchange of wealth, and credit was its product.

This inverted way of thinking was fundamental. It rationalized the delusion as a whole. Its most astonishing imaginary success was in the field of international finance, where it became unorthodox to doubt that by use of credit in progressive magnitudes to inflate international trade the problem of international debt was solved. All debtor nations were going to meet their foreign obligations from a favorable balance of trade.

A nation's favorable balance in foreign trade is from selling more than it buys. Was it possible for nations to sell to one another more than they bought from one another, so that every one should have a favorable trade balance? Certainly. But how? By selling on credit. By lending one another the credit to buy one another's goods. All nations would not be able to lend equally, of course. Each should lend according to its means. In that case this country would be the principal lender. And it was.

As American credit was loaned to European nations in amounts rising to more than a billion a year, in the general name of expanding our foreign trade, the question was sometimes asked: "Where is the profit in trade for the sake of which you must lend your customers the money to buy your goods?"

The answer was: "But unless we lend them the money to buy our goods they cannot buy them at all. Then what should we do with our surplus?"

As it appeared that European nations were using enormous sums of American credit to increase the power of their industrial equipment parallel to our own, all with intent to produce a great surplus of competitive goods to be sold in foreign trade, another question was sometimes asked: "Are we not lending American credit to increase Europe's exportable surplus of things similar to those of which we have ourselves an increasing surplus to sell? Is it not true that with American credit we are assisting our competitors to advance themselves against American goods in the markets of the world?"

The answer was: "Of course that is so. You must remember that these nations you speak of as competitors are to be regarded also as debtors. They owe us a great deal of money. Unless we lend them the credit to increase their power of surplus production for export they will never be able to pay us their debt."

Lingering doubts, if any, concerning the place at which a creditor nation might expect to come out, were resolved by an eminent German mind with its racial gift to subdue by logic all the difficult implication of a grand delusion. That was Doctor Schacht, formerly head of the German Reichsbank. He was speaking in this country. For creditor nations, principally this one, he reserved the business of lending credit through an international bank to the backward people of the world for the purpose of moving them to buy American radios and German dyes.

By this argument for endless world prosperity as a product of unlimited credit bestowed upon foreign trade, we loaned billions of American credit to our debtors, to our competitors, to our customers, with some beginning toward the backward people; we loaned credit to competitors who loaned it to their customers; we loaned credit to Germany who loaned credit to Russia for the purpose of enabling Russia to buy German things, including German chemicals. For several years there was ecstasy in the foreign trade. All the statistical curves representing world prosperity rose like serpents rampant.

Result: Much more debt. A world wide collapse of foreign trade, by far the worst since the beginning of the modern epoch. Utter prostration of the statistical serpents. Credit representing many hundreds of millions of labor days locked up in idle industrial equipment both here and in Europe. It is idle because people cannot afford to buy its product at prices which will enable industry to pay interest on its debt. One country might forget its debt, set its equipment free, and flood the markets of the world with cheap goods, and by this offense kill off a lot of competition. But of course this thought occurs to all of them, and so all, with one impulse, raise very high tariff barriers against one another's goods, to keep them out. These tariff barriers may be regarded as instinctive reactions. They do probably portend a reorganization of foreign trade wherein the exchange of competitive goods will tend to fall as the exchange of goods unlike and noncompetitive tends to rise. Yet you will be almost persuaded that tariff barriers as such were the ruin of foreign trade, not credit inflation, not the absurdity of attempting by credit to create a total of international exports greater than the sum of international imports, so that every country should have a favorable balance out of which to pay its debts, but only this stupid way of people all wanting to sell without buying.

The life history of delusions, how they get born, grow up, grow old and die, would be an interesting study. The beginning and growth of this one may be easily traced. War, discovery, and coincidence, all three, produced the occasion.

It took the war to discover in this country a power of production amazing to the world and no less to ourselves. We have forgotten how incredible it was. During the first few weeks of the war we were in a panic at the thought that to find money for their combat the nations of Europe might have to sell their holdings of American securities. If they were offered for sale on the New York Stock Exchange we should have to buy them.

Now, the total amount of Europe's holdings of American securities did not exceed $5 billion. Yet the prospect of having to repurchase five billion in American stocks and bonds from abroad was so terrifying that some of the elder international bankers in Wall Street proposed that this country should suspend gold payments. That is how little we knew of our own power. No one could have imagined that besides bailing our securities out of Europe, which we did on rising stock exchange quotations, we were about to spend $25 billion for participation in Europe's war and lend our European associates more than $10 billion at the same time—all in less than five years. To the world at large this was like the discovery of an infinitely rich new continent upon the explored earth; to us it was an astounding self-revelation.

The coincidence was that after many years of blundering toward it, and only a few months before the beginning of the war in Europe, we had found the formula for the most efficient credit machine that was ever invented. This was the Federal Reserve

System. The law creating it was enacted in December 1913. The extraordinary merit of the idea was that it contemplated for the first time a flexible currency to expand and contract in rhythm with the demands of trade and industry. Business to generate its own finance. That was the idea, and it worked. But as it worked that way, the credit resources of the old underlying national bank system and of the forty-eight separate state banking systems, hitherto employed to finance business through its seasons and cycles, were very largely released for other purposes, whatever they might be. Purposes of investment, promotion, and speculation.

The new order arrived just in time. Without it we should not have been able so easily to receive our securities back from Europe, nor to finance the war trade, nor to make those early private loans to the combatant nations. An Anglo-French loan for $500 million was the first notable test of its strength. And no sooner was it tried and found answerable in hundreds of millions than it had to be tested in tens of billions to finance the war loans of the United States government, borrowing both for itself and our European associates at the same time.

When the war was over this country was paramount in two dimensions. Its industrial power was apparently limitless, and it had the finest credit machine in the world. Certainly these ingredients were potent; and the road was strange.

It had long been the darling theme of a few world minds among us that as a people we should learn to "think internationally." We never had. Then suddenly we found ourselves in the leading international part, cast there by circumstances, with no experience, no policy rationally evolved, no way of thinking about it. To "think internationally," if it had ever been defined, was a way of thinking not of ourselves alone, but of others too, as all belonging to one world. In our anxiety to overtake this idea we overran it; international-mindedness became a way of thinking not of ourselves first but of the world first, of the other people in it, and of our responsibilities to them. No nation ever did think that way. If a nation did it would not long endure. To suppose this nation in its right mind could or would was the first sign of the oncoming delusion.

A variety of influences, incongruous among themselves, ran together to bring it on. There was the sentimental influence first. For nearly two years after the armistice the American goverment continued making loans to European countries for their general relief, extending them even to the side that was enemy, and did this with unlimited popular sanction. At the same time private assistance was offered and received on sentimental grounds. Societies were formed to adopt European towns and villages. The recovery of Europe was much more than our economic concern; we made it our emotional anxiety. Internationalism as a political cult seized the occasion to press its propaganda upon a receptive national mind. Friends of Europe organized themselves into eminent groups to support the European thesis for war debt cancellation at the expense of the American taxpayer. The direct influence of Europe was very powerful. In developing the thought of our unlimited moral and economic responsibility for the rehabilitation of Europe there was but one Old World voice; it spoke continually in all European languages, thus preparing, whether consciously or not, a fabulous source of credit. And at last American finance, as might have been foretold, went international, with a body of highly accented doctrine, some of it quite unsound, yet very appealing to the self-interest of American agriculture and American industry, both in a nightmare of surplus and easily persuaded that the only solution was in foreign trade, bought with American credit.

Neither agriculture nor industry cared how it was bought, only so long as some one else seemed to be paying for it. In the end everybody paid for it. The loss that fell upon the private investor fell also upon the whole country. Those foreign outlets for the surplus we were so anxious to get rid of turned out to be very costly.

To say there was no way with our surplus but to lend it away is simply to say that at this time our imagination failed. We kept thinking of surplus credit, and there is no such thing, short of total human satiety. That we had power to produce more food than we could eat ourselves, or more automobiles than we could use ourselves, was not a sign of surplus except in a particular, unimaginative sense. The power of production is in itself infinitely versatile. If there is more of it than we need to satisfy our immediate wants, then instead of using it to produce a surplus of goods to lend away in the foreign trade we may use it to perform prodigious collective works for the future. Or by economic and financial engineering we may convert it into credit and conserve it, as wild water is conserved, behind dams, against a time of famine. One way to convert and store it would be to pay off the public debt so that to meet any emergency thereafter the government should have a free, tremendous borrowing power, with no worry about its budget. But all the time it was easier to let it run away in happy torrents.

Obsessed with the thought of having a surplus of goods and a surplus of credit that we were obliged to lend, only to be rid of them, still there was no surplus in this country of good housing for people of low income in the cities. There was and is enormous need for such housing. The credit with which to meet it is difficult to command. Yet American credit was loaned freely to other countries for that purpose, notably to Germany. Capital borrowed on public credit to replace slum dwellings with model tenements may not be very profitable. It seldom is. But if we use our own capital for that purpose, even though it be lost, still we have the model tenements. If we build pyramids with our own credit at least we have the pyramids to enjoy; if we use our credit for works of private profit that turn out badly, the creditors who loaned the credit may send the sheriff to sell the property into new hands for what it will bring, and although we have wasted some credit, we have the externalized corporality of it entire.

But if we lend our credit to foreign countries and they build pyramids with it, we have to spend money in foreign travel even to look at them; and if we lend our credit for skyscrapers and railroads and power plants to be built in foreign countries and these turn out badly we cannot send the sheriff to seize them. Where is the state of Minas Geraes? You would not be expected to know. We loaned $16 million in American credit to the state of Minas Geraes, and all we know about it is that the bonds of Minas Geraes are in default. If Amarillo, Texas, had lost $16 million in American credit we should at least know where to go to look for it.

It is true that while what we called surplus American credit was vanishing abroad in sums rising to two billion a year, going to places we had never heard of and for purposes that sometimes were not even stated, public borrowing in the United States also was extravagant. Many cities and states were borrowing perhaps more than they could afford. Private borrowing in the United States at the same time may have been as reckless as private borrowing anywhere else. Say it was. There is still the difference between knowing and not knowing your debtor; between knowing and not knowing what he did with it, between the right of the creditor in his own country to lay hands on the property and his inability to act upon the news that his Brazilian bond is in default. He will receive the news by a printed form from the same American banking house that sold the bonds, now acting as Brazil's fiscal agent. Of the many Brazilian bonds floated in this country he may happen to have one of the issue named in the banker's prospectus: $25,000,000 United States of Brazil (Central Railway Electrification Loan of 1922) 30-year 7 percent Gold Bonds.'' The bonds are in default and the central railway was never electrified. What was done with the credit only Brazil knows. The bankers do not know. And what can be done about it is nothing.

The holder of a foreign bond must have bought it on faith. There was no other way. How could the individual investor examine for himself the economic resources of a foreign country and analyze its budget, or enter into the private accounts of a foreign corporation, try its balance sheet, and form a judgment, besides, of its prospects in the field?

On the science, wonder, and romance of American investments abroad, on the individual investor's perilous position in faith and on the moral responsibility of the banker, a very beautiful essay was written by the late Dwight W. Morrow, who had been a member of the house of J. P. Morgan and Company, international bankers; then ambassador to Mexico, later United States senator. It was printed in *Foreign Affairs,* an American quarterly of international vision, in the year 1927 (a year in which our loans to foreign countries exceeded the total borrowing of all American states, counties, townships, districts, towns, boroughs, and cities). This essay became at once a classic of the kind, referred to continually by all who wanted a theory or a philosophy of what we were doing. He was on a train, reading a Chicago newspaper, and he counted the foreign bonds listed in its daily bond table. The number was 128, where ten years before, as he learned by inquiry, there had been only 6. He wrote:

"Examining that long list of 128 bonds I discovered that governments, municipalities or corporations of some 30 different countries were represented—countries scattered all over the world. The list included the countries of our own hemisphere, Canada, Cuba, Brazil, Argentina, Chile, Peru, Bolivia, Uruguay; nations abroad with whom we fought and against whom we fought; governments in the Far East such as Japan and the Dutch East Indies; and cities as widely separated as Copenhagen and Montevideo, Tokyo and Marseilles.

"The contemplation of the extent and variety of America's investments in foreign bonds gives rise to three questions: Who buys these bonds? Why do they buy them? What do they get when they have bought them?"

These questions he set himself to answer. From statistical evidence he concluded that more than four buyers in every five were small investors and bought them in amounts from $100 up to $5,000. On this he said: "The investment in these foreign loans represents the savings of the person who spends less than he produces and thus creates a fund which he is able to turn over either to a domestic or to a foreign borrower.... When we talk about the person who is investing in foreign bonds we are not talking about a great institution in New York or Chicago or Boston. We are talking about thousands of people living in all parts of the United States. We are talking about schoolteachers and army officers and country doctors and stenographers and clerks."

Then the second question: Why do they buy foreign bonds? "Here," he wrote, "statistics are of little value.... The considerations in the minds of most investors are, first, the safety of the principal, and, second, the size of the interest yield. It should be borne in mind that the investor is the man who has done without something. He has done without something that he might presently have enjoyed in order that, in the future, his family may have some protection when he is gone, or in order, perhaps, that a son or a daughter may go to college. This investor wants to be certain that he will continue to receive income on the bond which he buys. He wants that income as large as is consistent with safety. Above all, he wants the principal returned to him on the day of the maturity of the bond. It cannot be asserted, however, that sentiment plays no part in our investments. It does. Many men in this country bought German bonds, after the successful launching of the Dawes Plan, not only because the rate of interest was attractive and the principal seemed secure, but because they felt that they were thus associating themselves in a fine venture to help Europe back on her feet." Sentiment allowed its due weight, yet Mr. Morrow supposed safety was always the first consideration. And he asked: "If that be true, how is the investor to form an intelligent judgment as to the safety of his investment? If he should be asked this question, I think that he would put in the very forefront of his reasons for making the investment the fact that he had confidence in the banker who offered him the investment. This throws a heavy responsibility upon the banker.''

Thirdly, the question: What does the buyer of a foreign bond get? On that he continued: "In 1924, 40 persons in a western city put $100 apiece into a Japanese bond maturing in 1954. What did those people get for their money? They got a promise. And, mark you, that promise was the promise of a group of people associated together on the other side of the earth. Moreover, so far as the promise relates to the payment of the principal of the bond, the promise does not mature in time to be kept by the particular members of the group who originally made it. It is a promise designed to be kept by the children of men now living. Yet somehow or other, the banker who offers that bond and the investor who buys that bond rely on the people of Japan taxing themselves a generation from now in order to pay back the principal of that bond to the children of the person who invests in the bonds today. At first blush it is a startling idea. It is particularly startling at this time when so many people are saying that the various nations of the earth have lost faith in each other. Here we have printed in a middle western newspaper the record of the day's dealings in 128 foreign bond issues. Individuals in America are taking their own money, with its present command over goods and services, and surrendering that command to nations on the other side of the earth, and they receive in exchange for it a promise. The question may be asked: Nothing more than a promise? to which the answer may be made: Nothing less than a promise.... Those nations who are borrowing in America because they actually need the money for a constructive purpose, who have a solidarity of national feeling and a sense of the meaning and value of national credit, who are not incurring obligations beyond what may fairly be considered their capacity to handle them—all those nations may be expected to pay their debts. Here again the responsibility rests heavily upon the investment banker recommending investments. The banker must never be lured, either by the desire for profit or the desire for reputation, to recommend an investment which he does not believe to be good.''

Two years later the crystal burst. Within four years the loss upon American investors abroad was incalculable.

Of the new Latin American bond issues that had been recommended to investors by the very best Wall Street banks and their bond-selling affiliates—of these alone, fifty-six issues, aggregating more than $800 million, were in default; and the fate of others not actually in default was very uncertain. In Europe, with a general moratorium on war debts and reparations, with a private moratorium running to Germany, another one to Austria, another one to Hungary, and with war debts and private debts involved in one great maelstrom of political controversy, the value of the American investment, present or ultimate, was very indefinite. Bonds of the German government selling on the New York Stock Exchange at thirty to sixty cents on the dollar, bonds of the state of Prussia at twenty-five cents, bonds of the city of Berlin at twenty cents, Hungarian bonds at fifteen to forty cents, many of the private bonds of European industry a little better or a little worse; and these were all bonds that had been eminently sold to the American investor within five or six years at ninety, ninety-five, and one hundred.

Then one by one the international bankers appeared before committees of inquiry of the United States Senate, all saying they thought the bonds were good and all alike disavowing further responsibility. They had not guaranteed the bonds or the validity of them. They were not responsible for how the money was spent or misspent; the borrowers were responsible. And as for the foreign bond delirium in this country, that was something the people, that is to say, the private investors, had done to themselves.

Before the Committee on Finance of the United States Senate, the head of the second largest national bank in Wall Street, who represented also the most aggressive bond-selling organization in the world, appeared and said: "We are merchants. With respect to bonds generally, we are merchants."

A member of the most powerful private international banking house said to the same committee: "We are merchants. That is what we are, just like any merchant, in the grain business, in the cotton business, or anything else."

The head of the largest national bank in Wall Street, one that owns also a very powerful bond-selling organization, appeared before the Senate Committee on Manufactures. The committee was hearing bankers on the question of establishing a national economic council and it was asking him what the bankers had done to restrain a wild use of American credit before the collapse. He said: "Speculation was in the air, and the speculators wanted to buy, buy, buy, and the bankers and brokers dealing in securities supplied that demand.... In other words, I do not think you would be justified in holding the bankers responsible for the wide speculative craze that worked through the country. I think they were trying to supply what the customers wanted.... I think the banker is like the grocer. He supplies what the customer wants."

And to that committee the head again of the second largest national bank in Wall Street, who appeared twice in Washington—looking at the same subject, namely, the delirious use of American credit in foreign securities—said: "It came about in part by reason of the public's interest in, and fever and fervor for, investments and speculation, if you will. It came about as a result of the demands of foreign countries for funds and an obvious appetite on the part of the American public for investment therein. The investment banking community became one of the tools by which the demands on each side operated to satisfy their requirements."

Grocers, merchants, and automatic tools. And the people Mr. Morrow wrote about all did it to themselves. Their sudden appetite for foreign bonds was so voracious that if they had read in every case the banker's prospectus, which few of them did, they perhaps would not have noticed the line in smaller type that always appeared at the bottom and read: "The information contained in this circular has been obtained partly from cable and other official sources. While not guaranteed, it is accepted by us as accurate."

Not even the accuracy of the information was guaranteed by the banker.

The Senate Committee on Finance learned a good deal about the merchant banker trade. It learned how foreign bonds originate in Wall Street and how they get from there to the hands of the individual investor. As in trade generally, there are parts, three at least and sometimes four, corresponding to the parts, respectively, of manufacturer, jobber, wholesaler, retailer.

There is first the bank that discovers and originates the bond issue. Let the borrower be a foreign government. The bank undertakes to buy from the foreign government so many bonds of a certain character at 90, and to pay for them on maybe the tenth day following the public offering. This originating bank then calls in a jobbing group of two or three banks of its own rank and says to them: "Here is a good thing. We will share it with you at 90½." So the jobbing group underwrites the bond issue at 90½, which is the first step-up. The jobbing group then forms a large syndicate of wholesalers, to whom it will sell the bonds at 92. This is the second step-up. The wholesalers know the retail trade; that is their business. Each wholesaler has a card index of retail bond dealers all over the country, with notations indicating about how many bonds of a certain kind each retailer may be expected to sell to the banks in his neighborhood and to the individual investors in his community. The wholesalers, by letter, telephone, and telegraph, offer this new bond to the retail trade at 94, which is the third step-up, and the retailers will sell them to the public at 96½, so that the retailer's profit will be 2½ percent, which is the last step-up.

When all these arrangements are made, the jobbing group advertises the bonds in the newspapers and at the same time establishes on the curb market, or over the bank counters, a public quotation a fraction above the retail price, say, 96 ⅝. This is the public offering. The originating house delivers the bonds to the jobbers, who deliver them to the wholesalers, who scatter them widely to the retail trade, and that day thousands of bond salesmen begin to solicit the small-town bank presidents and all the people Mr. Morrow wrote about, to buy the bonds. As the bonds are sold, the money starts moving from the many local sources toward Wall Street. Ten days after the public offering the wholesalers settle with the jobbers and the jobbers settle with the originating house and the foreign government gets its money. There are variations of the price steps, and, if the bond issue is small and juicy, the jobbers may go direct to the retail trade or the wholesalers themselves may perform the jobbing function, so that there may be only three steps instead of four; but with such slight modifications, the method as described is standard.

The only risk the Wall Street banker takes, you see, is in judging the public appetite. If his judgment is good the bonds are sold and paid for before the foreign government gets the money. The desirability of that result explains the speed and high tension at which all the machinery works.

All of that the committee could understand. Given the point of view of the international banker, that he is like a grocer, and then the uncontrollable demand on the part of the American public for his merchandise, it could understand why representatives of Wall Street banking houses went frantically to and fro in the world, pressing American credit upon foreign governments, foreign cities, foreign corporations, soliciting them to issue bonds to satisfy that American appetite; why at one time twenty-nine such representatives were all soliciting a small Latin American country to make a bond issue in Wall Street; even why American bankers paid large commissions, vulgarly mentioned as bribes, to influential private persons in foreign countries who could lead them to a new bond issue. It received with pleasure an acknowledgment of practical error from the head of a private banking house who said: "Yes, but it is also true that those things existed not only in Latin America, but the world over, relating to governments, municipalities and industrial concerns. In other words, the accumulation of capital in America was seeking an outlet. The bankers were the instruments of the outlet. They were the purveyors of capital. The bankers competed to a degree that in retrospect was wholly wrong. I am not speaking morally."

And yet all the simplicity of light that could be brought to bear upon these points seemed only more and more to obscure one another. The committee became very uneasy about it. Given again that inebriate demand on the part of the American investor which obliged the merchant banker to search the world for foreign borrowers, why then was it necessary for the bankers to adopt the intensive merchandising methods of industry in order to dispose of their merchandise? One would suppose it had sold itself, even faster than it could be originated. Why were foreign bonds so expensively advertised? Why were they pressed upon the investor through costly he-type selling organizations, by house-to-house canvass, even in some cases by radio ballyhoo? Questions to this point seemed always to embarrass the banker witnesses. The least indefinite answer either of the Senate committees got was made by the head of the foremost banking organization in Wall Street. He said: "Oh, undoubtedly salesmanship and advertising facilitate business; but you must remember that the banker cannot make that profit from his advertising and salesmanship unless the market is there to sell on, and unless the public is there to buy."

One point was too clear. There was no American policy. First and last, exclusive of the loans by United States government to its European war associates, private American credit to the incredible aggregate, roughly, of fifteen billion was loaned in foreign countries—without a policy.

If the State Department did touch foreign loans, it was with an ambiguous finger. Only once was the government openly positive, and that is how the State Department's contact with foreign loans began. When the United States Treasury stopped making post-armistice loans direct to European countries they all turned to Wall Street and began there to borrow private credit very heavily, while at the same time they were refusing to go to the United States Treasury and fund their promissory wartime notes into long-term bonds, according to the terms of their war loan contracts. So the government declared that it would disapprove of private American loans to foreign countries that were unwilling to honor their obligations to the United States Treasury. The government could not forbid their borrowing in Wall Street; it could only express its disapproval. But that was enough. All the debtor nations then came and did with their war debts at the United States Treasury what they had agreed to do.

Out of this arose the practice, which still continues, of referring a foreign loan to the State Department before it is publicly offered, to see if the government has any political objection to it. If there is none, the State Department says so and the bond issue proceeds; but what the State Department says is negative only, and confidential. When the State Department says there is no political objection to a foreign loan it does not thereby approve of the loan, or assume any moral responsibility whatever. The bankers understand this. Nevertheless, as it became generally known that all foreign bond issues were first referred to the State Department, the idea somehow grew up in the popular mind that they were issued under the sanction of the State Department, which was never so.

By informality the government did effectively object to a loan Wall Street would have floated for the Franco-German potash monopoly. The reasons were obvious to all but the bankers. Before the war this had been a Prussian monopoly. The whole world was dependent upon Germany for an indispensable plant food, a fact which entered deeply into the calculations of the German militarists as to how they should run the world after the German victory. But after the war France had the potash beds of Alsace, by cession of Alsace-Lorraine, whereupon the French and Germans agreed to handle potash as a joint monopoly and divided between them the markets of the world. During the war potash in this country went from $40 to $400 a ton because we were cut off from the German supply and our soil was starving for it. Only ten years later and with American chemical science struggling to develop American sources of potash as a vital national possession, Wall Street, but for the objection of the government, would have loaned $25 million in American credit to strengthen the Franco-German monopoly.

The enormous German borrowing in Wall Street, after the Dawes Plan loan, was a source of constant anxiety to the government, as it was to all observers whose motives were free and whose minds had not been seized by delusion. There was the danger, first, that if Germany's external private debts went on growing they would come into conflict with her reparation debts to France, Great Britain, Belgium, and others, as at last they did; and the danger, moreover, that such extravagant borrowing would bring Germany's whole financial structure to insolvency, as it did. Yet apparently there was nothing that could stop it.

S. Parker Gilbert, the American agent general for reparation payments, under the Dawes Plan, addressed a public protest to the German government, which he concluded by saying: "I have attempted to bring together in the foregoing pages the accumulating evidences of overspending and overborrowing on the part of the German public authorities, and some of the indications of artificial stimulation and overexpansion that are already manifesting themselves. These tendencies, if allowed to continue unchecked, are almost certain, on the one hand, to lead to severe economic reaction and depression, and are likely, on the other hand, to encourage the impression that Germany is not acting with due regard to her reparation obligations."

That made no difference. Wall Street ignored the warning. Again, writing from Paris to American bankers, November 3, 1926, Mr. Gilbert said: "I am constantly amazed at the recklessness of American bankers in offering to the public the securities of German States on the basis of the purely German view of Article 248 of the Treaty of Versailles. It is a simple matter, of course, to get letters from the financial authorities of the German States

setting forth the German point of view, and I can easily understand the willingness of the German authorities to sign letters
stating the German point of view, but it does seem to me difficult
to justify the action of the American bankers in offering the
securities to the public on the basis of such letters, without giving
the slightest hint that the German point of view is not accepted by
the Allied governments, and that, in fact, the Allied point of view
is diametrically opposed.''

Sir William Leese, of the Bank of England, supported Mr.
Gilbert with an analysis of the representations being made to
American investors in respect of two important German loans and
stated the following conclusion: ''Upon this point both prospec-
tuses are in my opinion substantially untrue and misleading.''
One for the city of Hamburg and one for the state of Prussia.

And that made no difference. The State Department, though
not objecting to any particular German loan, saying: ''. . . It cannot be said at this time that serious complications in connection
with interest and amortization payments by German borrowers
may not arise from possible future action by the agent general and
the transfer committee. . . . A further point which the department
feels should be considered by you. . . is the provision of Article
248 of the Treaty of Versailles, under which 'a first charge upon
all the assets and revenues of the German Empire and its constitu-
ent States' is created in favor of reparation and other treaty payments. . . . These risks, which obviously concern the investing
public, should in the opinion of the department be cleared up by
you before any action is taken. If they cannot be definitely elimi-
nated, the department believes that you should consider whether
you do not owe a duty to your prospective clients fully to advise
them of the situation.''

But so long as the government did not positively object, Wall
Street went on bringing out German bond issues, faster and faster
—the bonds of German states, German cities, German regions,
German industry, German agriculture, German ports, anything
German. Moreover, it kept hundreds of representatives in Germany soliciting all of these sources for bonds to sell to the American public.

In much of our lending to Europe, particularly as it ran to Germany, there was a sense of gesture. American credit was the rich
prodigal returning in a grand way from a far country to dazzle

and reward the indigent ancestor. And whether it was that some of the sentiment discovered by Mr. Morrow in his small investors worked itself up to the Wall Street mind, or that Wall Street itself needed emotional reasons and naturally acquired them, the fact is that bankers themselves became assertively sentimental about Germany. It is true that thinking of the effect of reparation payments upon the new German debt they were creating here might have inclined them realistically to the well-known German view of reparations; but they went much further and considered the effect of reparations upon the hearts and minds of Germans born since the war and of Germans yet unborn.

This was discovered to the Senate Committee on Finance by one of its most eminent banker witnesses, who said: "Here we have in Germany to-day young men going into the universities of Germany who were not born when the great war started. Those young men see that not only must they pay, but their progeny and the progeny of their progeny, must pay, and go on for these generations in paying a debt for which they, as individuals, were not responsible. They feel that they are under a heavy yoke, and my impression is that there is growing, as a result thereof, rebellion against payment of the debt."

Senator Reed asked this startling question: "Why should the progeny of Americans who had nothing to do with the war, the progeny of Americans who were not even alive, pay this war debt, and the progeny of the people who started it go scot free?"

The banker answered: "I grant you that that is quite unanswerable as an argument within itself."

If at any time you had asked an international banker to say whether or not there was an American policy to govern foreign loans he would have said yes, and if you had asked what it was, he would have said: "More and more our prosperity is and will be dependent on foreign trade. American loans abroad represent an investment in foreign trade."

This is not a policy. It is an idea only, largely fallacious as such. Here we have no state policy, as in France, that stipulates for political and economic advantages in return for credit loaned in other countries; nor is there here, as in England, the organized practice of tying up foreign loans with foreign contracts. American credit is loaned on the obscure presumption that trade will somehow follow; the borrowers, having got the credit, may do with it what they like.

Moreover, wherein our foreign loans do increase American exports, who is it that takes thought beforehand of how payment shall be received? Suppose the debtor offers to make payment in competitive goods that we do not want, and says he cannot pay in any other measure. That is happening. It is what is bound to happen when we lend American credit to foreign countries to increase their production of competitive goods; and the problem then is how we shall receive payment at all, if we keep a tariff against the exportable goods of our debtors.

But even that idea of buying foreign trade with American credit, to make outlets for the American surplus, was not consistently pursued. Take some typical instances.

With the American government borrowing credit to lend at low rates of interest to people who will build ships, thereby to foster an American merchant marine, American credit is loaned in large sums to German shipping companies; they use it to build German ships in German shipyards, with German labor and German materials, to compete with American ships.

With American chemical science dimly in sight of its goal, which is to make this country independent of Germany's synthetic chemistry, American credit is loaned to the German dye trust, whereby its offensive powers, in trade or in war, are strengthened.

If these are not cases in which we could not afford to lend American credit on any terms, still, where was the benefit to our own foreign trade? Lending very large sums of American credit to the Anglo-Chilean nitrate trust does neither increase the volume of American exports nor foreshorten the time in which we may hope by synthetic chemistry to free ourselves from dependence upon foreign sources of nitrogenous fertilizers and the essential chemical products of nitrate; and the same is to be said of loans of American credit to German and Italian corporations for the purpose of building nitrogen fixation plants. Lending $40 million of American credit to a foreign oil company, for drilling and exploration, can hardly be called an investment in our own foreign trade, nor a loan of $150 million of American credit to the Dutch East Indies to pay off its floating debt. It would be difficult to explain how lending large sums of American credit to the fabulous

Swedish match trust, which in turn made loans to European governments in exchange for monopolistic trade concessions, benefited the sale of American goods in the foreign trade. Certainly a loan of American credit to a Latin American republic to pay a debt it owed in Europe for armament had no beneficial trace in the American foreign trade. Or fancy any benefit to the American export trade from a loan of $20 million to a German bank for the specific purpose, as stated by the bankers, "to finance German exporting corporations."

Glance at the contradiction of lending very large sums of American credit for the purpose of extending, improving and financing Europe's agriculture, with the American government borrowing credit to support the price of American wheat because the European demand for American grain declined. The word for this may be one of unction or it may be cynical, from opposite points of view, but certainly there was no policy in it. If for any reason we were going to lend our credit to extend Europe's agriculture, we should have been providing at the same time both the credit and the economic engineering to shrink American agriculture proportionately, without disaster to the farmer.

Loans to Europe, especially to Germany, to rationalize industry and introduce American methods of mass production could benefit American industry in the foreign trade only if you argued that what American industry needed for its own good was more competition.

But of all the ways in which the lending of American credit in Europe did not increase the American export trade, the one most extraordinary was that of lending our debtors the credit with which to make payment to us on their debt. American loans to Germany enabled Germany to pay reparations to the Allies; reparations from Germany enabled the Allies to pay interest on their war debts at the United States Treasury, hardly touching their own pockets. We were paying ourselves. For a long time this simple construction was denied and concealed in the elaborate confusions of finance. The Senate Committee on Finance kept asking its banker witnesses to face it. One of the best answers was by Otto H. Kahn, who said:

"There is no doubt that if Germany had not been able to borrow money it would have been unable, long since, to pay reparations, and, therefore, to that extent, it is a generally correct statement to say that out of the money which Germany borrowed it did pay reparations.''

Then at last the German government itself, to prove Germany's incapacity to pay, publicly declared that reparations had been paid only by borrowing and that if Germany could not continue to borrow she could not continue to pay.

That debt need never be paid, that it may be infinitely postponed, that a creditor nation may pay itself by progressively increasing the debts of its debtors—such was the logic of this credit delusion.

Since John Law and his Mississippi Bubble, individuals have been continually appearing with the same scheme in new disguise. The principle is very simple. You have only to find a way to multiply your creditors by the cube and pay them by the square, out of their own money. Then for a while you are Nabob. One fish cut up for bait brings 3. Two of these cut up for bait bring 8, the cube of 2. Four of these cut up for bait bring 64, the cube of 4. Sixteen of these for bait bring 4,096, and 256 of these, which is the square of 16, will bring 16,777,216, which is the cube of 256.

The fatal weakness of the scheme is that you cannot stop. When new creditors fail to present themselves faster than the old creditors demand to be paid off, the bubble bursts. Then you go to jail, like Ponzi, or commit suicide, like Ivar Kreuger.

There is nothing new in the scheme. What is new is that for the first time the whole world tried it. The whole world cannot put itself in jail, nor can it escape the consequences by suicide.

When the delusion breaks, people all with one impulse hoard their money, banks all with one impulse hoard credit, and debt becomes debt again, as it always was. Credit is ruined. Suddenly there is not enough for everyday purposes. Yet only a little while before we had been saying and thinking there was a great surplus of American credit and the only thing we could do with it was to export it. How absurd it sounds in echo. It was absurd at the time.

Our problem properly was, properly is, for a long time will be, how to find enough credit to perform the works that lie ahead of us, only such as are in sight. We already see that we shall have to recast the entire transportation machine, wherein is to be faced both a terrific loss of old capital and the necessity to provide in place of it enormous sums of new capital. We already know that we shall have to relate and organize in a rational manner our sources of energy by bringing the three hydrocarbons, coal, gas, and oil, into a few immense pools, where they may be converted interchangeably into forms ideal for the several needs of life, industry and commerce, and whence they may be distributed, without waste, more and more efficiently, until fuel, heat, light, and power shall become as cheap as water. We have our cities to make over, not to meet their future, but only to accommodate the change that has already occurred in the patterns and conditions of American life. There is no suburban area but must be reclaimed from its anarchy of free growth and recast to a regional plan by colossal engineering.

The new materials and methods discovered almost daily by science are creating obsolescence at a rate never before imagined. Notwithstanding the physical progress everywhere to show, the fact is that in contrast with the present state of technical and scientific knowledge and the power we possess, the country is more in arrears than it was a generation ago; it has much more to overtake. Many of the blueprints are ready and fading for want of credit.

Anatomy of the Bubble

Who, then, is he who provides it all? Go and find him and you will have once more before you the Forgotten Man.... The Forgotten Man is delving away in patient industry, supporting his family, paying his taxes, casting his vote, supporting the church and the school, reading his newspaper, and cheering for the politician of his admiration, but he is the only one for whom there is no provision in the great scramble and the big divide.

— WILLIAM GRAHAM SUMNER

Command of labor and materials built the pyramids. The economic world was then very simple. Some private usury, of course, but no banking system, no science of credit, no engraved securities issued on the pyramids for investors to worry about. Merely, the whim of Pharaoh, his idea of a pyramid, his power to move labor, and the fact of a surplus of food enough to sustain those who were diverted from agriculture to monumental masonry.

It is believed that on Cheops alone 100,000 men were employed for twenty years. And when it was finished all that Egypt had to show for 600 million days of human labor was a frozen asset. Otherwise and usefully employed, as, for example, upon habitations and hearthstones, works of common utility, means of national defense, that amount of labor might have raised the standard of common living in Egypt to a much higher plane, besides insuring Egyptian civilization a longer competitive life. But once it had been spent on a pyramid to immortalize the name of Pharaoh it was spent forever. People could not consume what their own labor had produced. That is to say, they could not eat a pyramid, or wear it, or live in it, or make any use of it whatever. Not even Pharaoh could sell it, rent it, or liquidate it.

History does not say what happened to the 100,000 when Cheops was finished. Were they unemployed? Were they returned to agriculture whence they came? If so, that would be like now sending suddenly four or five million people from industry back to the farms in this country.

You may take it, at any rate, that when Cheops was finished, there occurred in Egypt what we should call an economic crisis, with no frightful statistics, no collapsing index numbers in the daily papers, no stock-exchange panic, no bank failures, but with unemployment, blind social turmoil, Egyptian bread lines perhaps. And this crisis, like every crisis since, down to the very last, was absorbed by people who could not consume what they had produced, whose labor had been devoured by a pile of stones, and who understood it dimly if at all. The forgotten people.

This story of a pyramid has the continuing verity of a parable. For all the worlds that have passed since that Egyptian civilization departed, for all the new wonders of form, method, and power that seem to make this one of ours original, nevertheless, what happened to the forgotten people of Egypt happens still in our scheme; it happens to The Forgotten man of William G. Sumner's classic essay, and for the same reasons.

There is here no solitary Pharaoh with the power to move labor by word alone. In this world labor is free, receiving wages. Yet you have to see that the passion among us for individual and collective aggrandizement by command of labor and materials is what it always was and that the consequences of pursuing it far in selfish and uneconomic ways are what they are bound to be and anciently were.

In place of one responsible Pharaoh at a time, we have a multitude of irresponsible Pharaohs; and beyond these we have the Pharaoh passion acting in governments big and little, in states and cities, in great private and public organizations, all seeking their own exaggeration and all seeking it by the one means. The motive may be avarice, it may be good or bad, it may derive from a sense of rivalry between nations or from an idea of public happiness. In the nature of economic consequences, strange to say, the motive does not matter. A pyramid is a pyramid still. When too much labor has been spent upon pyramids, or things that are unproductive and dead in the economic meaning of pyramids, there will be a crisis in daily well-being, and free labor in that case will be as helpless as slave labor was. It cannot consume what it has produced; it is without all those human satisfactions that might have been produced with the same labor in place of the pyramid, and it is without them forever. The labor that is lost cannot be recovered by unbuilding the pyramid.

But in this world where labor is free and no one has the apparent power to move it beyond its own volition, how is it moved or procured to waste itself too far upon works of public and private aggrandizement? How now do we build pyramids? There is a new way. It is a way the ancients, the Pharaohs, with no science of banking, could not have imagined. The name of it is credit. In our world, a world of money economy, command of credit is the command of labor and materials. There may be intervening complexities, the obvious may be obscured, yet in every case that is what it comes to at last; and, in fact, people have no other use for credit.

Borrowing and lending are as old as the sense of mine and thine; therefore, so is credit in the simple term. But modern credit as we know it, or think we know it, is a new and amazing power, still evolving, still untamed. Men have been much more anxious to release the power of credit, to employ and exploit it, than to control it or even to understand it. That would be only human. As formerly there was no aggrandizement, private or public, without a Pharaoh-like command of labor and materials, so now there is none without command of credit.

This holds for aggrandizement in any dimension. The very

magnitude of human life in the present earth is owing to the power of credit. The whole of our industrial phenomena is founded on it. By means of credit the machine is created in the first place; by means of credit the machine is manned and moved and fed with raw materials. By means of credit the product of machines is distributed. By means of credit more and more this product is consumed, as when credit is loaned at home to the installment buyer or loaned abroad to the foreign customer. Thus the power of credit is employed dynamically in the aggrandizement of trade, wherein are many dangers yet to be explored, such as those of wild inflation and deflation, followed by sudden crisis. The greed of individuals and groups, the extravagances of civic ego, the ambition of nations, ideas creative and destructive both, great social ends and great fallacies at the same time, even war—credit for all of these is the fabulous agent. And then, besides, with any motive, it builds pyramids, which is the singular point and the one we are after.

That is the one thing credit is supposed not to do. The restraining principles are interest and amortization. To amortize a debt is to redeem it, to extinguish it finally, or, literally, put it to death. Debt we have not mentioned. Most of the follies we commit with the power of credit are from forgetting that debt is the other face of credit. There is no credit but with an exact equivalent of debt. That is to say, when by means of credit you command labor and materials, you borrow them and become a debtor. As a debtor you must pay interest, so much per annum, on what you have borrowed, and sometime later return the principal, which puts the debt to death. We suppose commonly that interest and amortization concern only the borrower and lender. Who lends money will demand something for the use of it while he himself is doing without it, and surety for its return after a certain time. That is so; but that is not all of it.

From the point of view of the total social organism, interest and amortization have a kind of functional significance. They are the only two checks we have upon the universal passion to abuse the power of credit, or to waste in reckless and uneconomic ways the labor that is by credit commanded.

The borrower is expected to say: "This thing I propose to create with credit will be in turn creative. I mean it will be productive and give increase. Out of the increase I will pay interest for use of the credit; out of the increase I will extinguish the debt. The remainder I will keep for my own as profit.''

He may say that of a steel works, a textile factory, a railroad, an electric power plant, of ten thousand and one things you may not think of; he cannot say it of a pyramid.

Precisely, therefore, the function of interest and amortization, beyond any private concern of either borrower or lender, is to restrain pyramid building. Nevertheless, it will be perceived that the modern world is magnificent with pyramids. Where Pharaoh built one by tyrannical command of labor and materials, credit now builds thousands. You are not to look for them in the exact shape of Pharaoh's. Ours are in shapes of endless variety, many of them apparent, some not so apparent because they present a specious aspect of usefulness, and some invisible. The invisible kind are of all the most devouring.

Taking them by kinds, what are they—our pyramids? The most obvious to perception are those in the category of public works, such as monumental buildings, erections to civic grandeur, ornate boulevards, stadiums, recreation centers, communal baths, and so on. Here, to begin with, the restraining function of interest and amortization is relaxed. It is not said that works in this character will be productive. It is said that they will contribute to the happiness and comfort of people, which is their justification, and it is generally true. And it is said, moreover: "Why should people wait until they can have saved the money for this extension of their happiness and comfort when they may have it immediately on credit? They will tax themselves to pay interest on the debt and to pay the principal of the debt as it comes due."

But so even with pyramids in this very desirable meaning, let the impatience for them become extravagant and reckless, as it will and does, and let too much labor be moved by credit to the making of them all at once, and you may be sure of what will happen. To pay interest on the debt and then to pay the debt itself taxes will rise until people cannot afford to pay them. That is what they will say. But the reason they cannot afford to pay taxes is that they could not afford those very desirable unproductive things to begin with. Either they did not know this in time or they did not care. They may repudiate the debt, yet as you may consider society in the whole that will make no difference whatever, since it remains true that society in the whole is wanting all those

51489

other exchangeable human satisfactions, more important than sights and diversions, that might have been produced with the same labor in place of those well-intentioned and premature pyramids.

In another category are things that afterward turn into pyramids. This will happen when those by whom the credit was commanded have used it with bad judgment, or too much of it for a given result, or dishonestly, or to create a thing for which after all there is no demand, so that what they were pursuing was not a reality within reason of probability but a delusion of profit—and pursuing it with other people's labor, other people's money. Yet the thing itself may be magnificent, like the tallest skyscraper in a great city, so marvellous in its architectural and engineering features that people will come from great distances away for the thrill of looking at it. Whether or not in such a case given, the entire motive was profit, free of any will to aggrandizement, it is profit or loss that will determine the economic status of each new piece of wonder. If there is profit, if it can pay interest and put the debt to death out of its earnings, or, that is to say, if it can return to the common reservoir the credit that was borrowed, then it is not a pyramid. It is a thing productive, giving increase. But if there is loss, so that interest and amortization cannot be met out of the increase, out of the earnings, out of the rents, then and exactly in the measure to which this is true, the thing is a pyramid. We say in that case the capital is lost. But what the loss of capital means is that the labor is lost, and again, no matter who specifically takes the loss, society as a whole is wanting all the imaginable other satisfactions that might have been produced in place of this pyramid.

By the same definition, the overbuilding of industry beyond any probable demand for the product represents devoured credit. Here the spirit of aggrandizement acts as if it were a biological law, each separate organization trying to outgrow all the others of its own kind in the industry of one country, and then that industry as a whole in one country trying to outgrow the competitive industry of another country, and this going on with benefit of more and more credit, until at last—what is the problem? The problem is that so much credit, that is to say labor, is trapped, frozen, locked up in the world's industrial machine, that people cannot afford to buy the whole of its product at prices which will enable industry to pay interest on its debt. This is perhaps the most involved form of pyramid that human ingenuity has yet devised.

To see it clearly, you may have to push it to the focus of extreme absurdity. Suppose, for example, that half of all the capital in the world were invested in shoemaking machinery. You have there the capacity to make in one day many more shoes than there are feet in the world, and yet the necessity to pay interest on half the capital in the world and charge it to the price of shoes will make shoes so dear that nobody can afford to buy them. The answer is that all the capital invested in excess shoemaking machinery is lost. Nearly half the capital in the world! Half less the relatively small amount that may be properly so invested. Exactly. It is really lost. The labor it represents is lost. All the wanted things that this labor might have produced in place of that excess of shoemaking machinery—they are lost, and forever lost. You cannot recover the labor by unbuilding the machinery any more than Pharaoh could have recovered his wasted Egyptian labor by unbuilding the pyramid.

Then the invisible pyramids—what are they?

A delirious stock-exchange speculation such as the one that went crash in 1929 is a pyramid of that character. Its stones are avarice, mass delusion, and mania; its tokens are bits of printed paper representing fragments and fictions of title to things both real and unreal, including title to profits that have not yet been earned and never will be. All imponderable. An ephemeral, whirling, upside-down pyramid, doomed in its own velocity. Yet it devours credit in an uncontrollable manner, more and more to the very end; credit feeds its velocity.

In two years brokers' loans on the New York Stock Exchange alone increased $5 billion. That was credit borrowed by brokers on behalf of speculators, and it was used to inflate the daily Stock Exchange quotations for those bits of printed paper representing fragments and fictions of title to things both real and unreal. It was credit that might have been used for productive purposes. The command of labor and materials represented by that amount of credit would have built an express highway one hundred feet wide from New York to San Francisco and then one from Chicago to Mexico City, with something over. Or taking wages at six dollars a day, it represents more than the 600 million days of man power wasted by Pharaoh on his Cheops. But the use of it to inflate Stock Exchange prices added not one dollar of real wealth to the country.

You may think that since it was all a delusion on the profit side, the loss also must have been imaginary; that if nothing was added to the wealth of the country, neither was anything taken away. But that is not the way of it. First there was the direct loss of diverting that credit from all the possible uses of production to the unproductive use of speculation. Secondly, a great deal of it was consumed by two or three million speculators, large and small, who, with that rich feeling upon them, borrowed money on their paper profits and spent it. In this refinement of procedure what happens is that imaginary wealth is exchanged for real wealth; and the real wealth is consumed by those who have produced nothing in place of it. Thirdly—and this was the terrific loss—the shock from the headlong fall of this pyramid caused all the sensitive sources and streams and waters of credit to contract in fear. The more they contracted the more fear there was, the more fear the more contraction, effect acting upon cause. The sequel was abominable panic.

This is only the most operatic example of the pyramid invisible. Such a thing must be any artificial or inflated price structure, requiring credit to support it. The Federal Farm Board built two great pyramids in agriculture, one in wheat and one in cotton, and named them stabilization. It was using government credit, borrowed from the people, to support wheat and cotton prices. Nevertheless, wheat and cotton prices were bound to fall, and that credit was lost. There has been a vogue for pyramids by the name of stabilization. Scores of them have been built, private and public, all using credit in a more or less desperate effort to support prices that were bound for natural reasons to fall.

Foreign trade inflated by the credit we loaned to our foreign customers—that was a grand pyramid of a special kind, half visible and half invisible, partly real and partly unreal. The trade was visible; the idea of profit in it was largely a delusion. Almost we forgot that we were buying this trade with our own credit.

Moreover, of total loans out of the American credit reservoir to foreign countries, amounting grossly to $15 billion, a great deal of it has been used not to inflate foreign trade but by the foreign borrowers to build pyramids of their own at our expense. This magnificent oddity, here only to be mentioned, will return in its due place.

A certain confusion may now be beginning to rise. Credit, again, regarded simply as a command of labor and materials. In that definition the mind makes no difficulty about relating it to ponderable things, such as pyramids in the form of public works or excess industrial capacity, for these are only certain physical objects in place of others that might have been wrought with the instrumentality of that same credit; it may, however, find some difficulty in relating it to imponderable things also called pyramids, such as a Wall Street ecstasy. For how does credit originate? Whose is it to begin with? How is command of it acquired? How does it get from where it originates to where it is found producing its prodigious effects?

All of this may be seen, and will be easier to do than you would think. To see credit rising at its source, to see whose it is to begin with, to see how it moves from the spring to the stream and then anywhere, even to the maelstrom, and to see at the same time Sumner's Forgotten Man, you have only to go to the nearest bank and sit there for half an hour in an attitude of attention. Any bank will do. The first one you come to.

Observe first the physical arrangements. There will be along the counter a series of little windows, each with a legend over it. Above one window it will be "Savings." Over the next two or three it will be "Teller." Then one, "Discounts and Collections." And at one side, where the counter ends, you will see behind a railing several desks with little metal plates on them, one saying "President," another "Vice-President," and another "Cashier," unless it is a very small bank, in which case the cashier will be behind one of the windows.

Then observe the people and what they come to do. Some go straight to the window marked "Savings." These all bring money to leave with the bank at interest. One is a man in overalls. That is wage money to be saved. Another is a farmer's wife, and that may be milk or butter money. Next the poultry man with some profit to be put aside. Then two or three housewives, evidently, such as regularly include in their budgets a sum to be saved. After these a foreman from the railroad and a garage mechanic, and so on. Each one puts money between the leaves of a little book and pushes it through the window; the man there counts it, writes the amount in the little book and pushes the book back to the depositor. That goes on all day. At the day's end all the money received at this window is counted, bundled and tossed into the safe, and then written down in the big book of the bank as "Time Deposits."

Those who go to the windows marked "Teller" are somewhat different. They represent local trade, commerce, and industry. Their accounts are current, called checking accounts or credit balances. They bring both cash and checks to deposit; and besides making deposits they may tender their own checks to be cashed, often at the same time. For example, the man who owns the sash and blind factory brings nothing but checks to deposit; everybody owing him money has paid him by check. But he hires ten men and this is payday. Therefore, needing cash to pay wages, he writes his own check for the amount of his pay roll and receives that sum in cash. But this money he takes away presently comes back to the bank through other hands. The employees of the sash and blind factory spend it with the grocer and butcher and department-store keeper who immediately bring it to the bank and deposit it at the "Teller" windows where it came from. What the employees of the sash and blind factory do not spend they themselves bring back to the bank and leave at the window marked "Savings." Such is the phenomenon called the circulation of money. The same dollar may go out of the bank and return again two or three times in one week. The speed with which a dollar performs its work and returns to the bank is called the velocity of money.

At the end of the day the men at the "Teller" windows count up in one column what they have received and in another what they have paid out, and the difference is written down in the bank's books as an increase or decrease of "Demand Deposits." The rule is that more will have been received than was paid out, so there is normally each day an increase of deposits. It is normal that all these people representing local business should bring to the "Teller" windows more than they take away, because their activities are severally productive, giving always some increase, more or less according to the state of the times.

Well, then, this daily increase of "Demand Deposits" from the "Teller" windows is tossed into the safe, along with those "Time Deposits" from the window marked "Savings." Thus the bank accumulates deposits—that is to say, money. What does it do with the money? A bank pays interest; therefore, a bank must earn interest. It must earn more interest than it pays out, else it cannot make a profit for itself. So the bank must lend its deposits. To receive money on which it pays interest and to lend money on which it receives interest—that is a bank's whole business.

Now, what proportion of its total deposits do you suppose a bank lends? How much would you think it was safe to lend? The half? Three-quarters? All? The fact is—and even those who know it well and take it for granted are astonished in those moments when they stop to reflect on it—the fabulous fact is that a bank may lend ten times its deposits. That is to say, for each actual dollar of other people's money it has received and locked up in its safe, it may lend or sell ten dollars of credit money.

Not every bank does lend ten to one—ten dollars of credit to one of cash in the vault; but if you take the banking system entire it has the potential power to erect credit in that ratio to cash. Ten to one was the formula adopted by the United States Treasury and other federal government agencies in their campaign against hoarding. In official messages broadcast over the country people were exhorted to stop hoarding and bring their money back to the banks on the ground that each dollar of actual money in hiding represented a loss of ten in the credit resources in the country, and that each dollar of money brought back to the banks represented an increase of ten dollars in credit for the common benefit of trade, commerce and industry.

The beginning of all modern credit phenomena is in this act of multiplication, performed by the banker. How can a bank lend credit to the amount of ten times its cash deposits?

Perhaps the easiest way to explain it will be to tell the story of the old goldsmiths who received gold for safe keeping and issued receipts for it. These receipts, representing the gold, began to pass from hand to hand as money. Seeing this, and that people seldom touched the gold itself or wanted it back, so long as they thought it was safe, the goldsmiths began to issue paper redeemable in gold, without having the gold in hand to redeem it with. A very audacious idea. And yet it was sound, or at least it worked, and if a goldsmith was honest he was solvent because in exchange for that paper, which he promised to redeem in gold on demand, he took things of value, called collateral, in pledge, so that against his outstanding paper he had good assets in hand, and if people did come with his paper, wanting the gold on it, he had only to sell those assets, buy the gold, then redeem the paper according to his promise—always provided the assets were liquid and easily sold and that too many people never came at once, all demanding gold on the instant. Fewer and fewer people ever did want the actual gold. So long as they believed in the goldsmith they preferred to use his paper for all purposes of exchange—paper which no longer represented the actual gold and yet was as good as gold and was counted as gold because whenever anybody did want the gold it was forthcoming. From this evolved modern banking. That circulating paper itself became legal money against which the banks were obliged by law and custom to keep a certain amount of gold in hand, called the gold reserve. The next step was to discover that upon this structure of legal paper money with a gold reserve behind it you could impose another strata of paper—a new free kind, redeemable either in gold or legal paper money. That new free kind of paper was the bank check we all know; and the use of bank checks in place of actual money has increased by habit and necessity until now we transact more than nine-tenths of all our business by check, no actual money passing at all, or almost none. In the year 1929, for example, the total amount of actual money of all kinds in the country was $9 billion; but the total exchange of bank checks was $713 billion, or nearly eighty times all the actual money in existence.

What a bank now lends is credit in the form of a blank checkbook. You use the credit by writing checks against it. You may write a check for cash and draw out actual money in the form of gold or legal paper money, but if you do and spend the money it will go straight back to the bank. When you borrow at the bank, what happens? The banker does not hand you the money. He writes down in the bank's own book a certain credit to your account and gives you a book of blank checks. Then you go out and begin to write checks against that credit. The people to whom you give the checks deposit them in the bank. As they deposit your checks the sums are charged to your account, deducted from your credit on the books. No actual money is involved.

If these last few passages have been difficult, take the fact lightly and without blame. Of all the discoveries and inventions by which we live and die this totally improbable helix of credit is the most cunning, the most liable, the least comprehended, and, next to high explosives, the most dangerous. All that bankers themselves really know about it is how it works from day to day. Beyond that it is a gift from Pandora.

But you are still sitting in the local bank. Take it, if necessary, as an arbitrary fact that for each dollar of actual money that passes inward through those windows and stops in the safe the bank will have six, eight, maybe ten dollars of credit to lend. To whom does it lend this credit? And how?

There is a window yet to be observed, the one marked "Discounts and Collections." The transactions at this window take more time. Papers are signed and exchanged. These people are borrowers; they are attending to their loans, paying them off, or paying something on account, or arranging to have their promissory notes extended. One is the local contractor who has had to have credit on his note to pay for materials and labor while building a house; the house is finished, he has been paid by the owner, and now he returns the credit by paying off his note—with a check. Another is the local automobile dealer who has just received from Detroit a carload of automobiles with draft attached, and the draft reads, "Pay at once." To pay the draft he must borrow credit at the bank; as he sells the automobiles one by one in the community he will return the credit—by check. Another is the radio dealer who sells radios on the installment plan. He is borrowing credit against which he will write a check to pay the radio manufacturer for ten sets; as security for the loan he gives his own promissory note, together with the ten purchase contracts of the ten local people to whom he has sold the radio sets. As they pay him he will pay the bank—by check. Another is a farmer who has sold his crop and now is paying back—by check—the credit he borrowed six months ago to buy fertilizer and some new farm machinery.

Lending of this character, to local people, the bank knowing all of them personally, is not only the safest kind of lending for the bank; it is the ideal use of credit. Unfortunately, the local demand for credit is not enough to absorb the bank's whole lending power. From the savings of the community, always accumulating in the safe as cash deposits, the bank acquires a surplus lending power. Having satisfied its own customers with credit at the window marked "Discounts and Collections," what will the bank do with the surplus credit? Well, now you will see how credit, so rising at the obscure local source, overflows the source and begins to seek outlets to the lakes and gulfs and seas beyond—how its adventures begin.

The first thing the bank thinks to do with a part of its surplus credit is to lend it to a big New York City bank.

What will the New York bank do with it? The New York bank may lend it to a merchant in domestic trade or to one in the foreign trade; it may lend it to a broker on the Stock Exchange who lends it to a speculator; it may lend it in Europe to the Bank of England or it may lend it to a German bank where the interest rate is very high. Fancy local American credit, originating as you have seen, finding its way from this naive source to a Berlin bank! Well, several hundreds of millions of just that kind of American credit did find its way to the banks of Germany and got trapped there in 1931. The German banks said they could not pay it back. That was what the moratorium was all about. Germany said if we insisted on having our credit back, her banks would simply shut up; she advised us to "freeze" it and leave it there on deposit in the German banks, in the hope that they might be able later to pay, and since there was nothing else to do we did that.

What else will the local bank do with its surplus credit? It will buy a United States government bond; it is simply lending this credit to the federal government.

What will the federal government do with it? The federal government may give it to the Federal Farm Board to support those wheat and cotton pyramids; the federal government may give it to the Reconstruction Finance Corporation, which will lend it to the railroads; the federal government may give it to the Veterans' Bureau, which will lend it to war veterans, or the federal government may spend it either to finish the memorial bridge across the Potomac River at Washington or for paper and lead pencils to be distributed on the desks of the Senate and House.

But the local bank has still a surplus of credit to lend. So far, by all the rules, it has been very conservative. The credit it has loaned to the big New York City bank is returnable on call. No worry about that. To get back the credit it has loaned to the United States government it has only to sell the bond, and there is always an instant market for government bonds. So now the bank thinks it may take some risk, for the sake of obtaining a higher rate of interest.

You may notice a man talking very earnestly to the president at the desk behind the railing, and from something you read in his gestures you may take him to be a salesman. That is what he is—a bond salesman from Wall Street, and his merchandise this time is foreign bonds. He has some South American government bonds that pay seven percent and some German municipal bonds that pay eight percent, and these are very attractive rates of interest, seeing that the bank pays its depositors only three and one-half.

"You may think," the salesman is saying to the president, "that such rates of interest as seven and eight percent imply some risk in these bonds. Really there is no risk. The bonds are absolutely good. Foreign borrowers have to pay high rates of interest in this country, not because they are anything but good and solvent borrowers, but because our people are strange to foreign investments. That being temporarily so, this is a rare opportunity for a little bank like yours to make some very profitable investments."

So persuaded, the local bank with the remainder of its surplus credit buys foreign bonds. When it buys the bond of a South American government, it is lending credit to that government, knowing no more about it than the salesman says. What will the South American government do with that credit? Anything it likes, because it is a sovereign government; it may use it to build a gilded dome. Many new gilt domes have been built in foreign countries with just this kind of local American credit.

In buying the German bonds the bank is lending credit to the free city of Bremen, perhaps, or to Cologne. What does the free city of Bremen do with it? She may use it to widen the fairway of her harbor and build some new piers. The same credit might have been used to make ship channels and piers in the Hackensack Meadows of New Jersey. And what does Cologne do with it? She may use it to build a stadium or a great bathing pavilion for the happiness and comfort of her people. How strange! The local American community out of which this credit rises to perform such works in Germany has neither stadium nor swimming pool of its own. Or Cologne may use it to help build the largest new bridge in Europe across the Rhine, a bridge she really does not need, except to provide employment for her people. The same credit might be used to build a bridge across the Golden Gate at San Francisco.

One last observation before you leave the bank. How remote these people are from what is doing with the credit that rises from the dollars they leave at the windows! How little they know about it! Fancy telling that woman at the "Savings" window, who gets her money up in small bills from the deeps of an old satchel, that her dollars, multiplied ten times by the bank, will go to build ornaments for a grand boulevard in a little Latin American country she never heard of, or to build workmen's houses in a German city better than the house she lives in. Fancy telling the man in overalls who comes next that his money, multiplied ten times by the bank, will go to a speculator on the New York Stock Exchange, or to mend a cathedral in Bavaria, or to a foreign bank that may lose it unless the matter of reparations is somehow settled in Europe, or that it may be loaned to Germany in order that Germany may pay reparations to the Allies in order that they may be willing to pay something on account of what they owe to the United States Treasury.

Remember as you leave the bank that it was one of 25,000, big and little, all performing the same act of multiplication, all in the same general ways lending the product of multiplication, which is credit. You have seen only one spring in the woods. Think of 25,000 such springs in the land, all continually overflowing with credit, and how this surplus local credit, seeking interest, by a law as unerring as the force of gravity finds its way to the streams that lead away to the lakes, gulfs, and seas beyond. If you will keep this picture in suspense, you will better understand what else happens, if and when it does—and it is bound to happen from a reckless or deluded use of the power of credit.

There is a change in the economic heavens. Some stars fall out. On the ground some pyramids collapse. For two or three weeks what the Wall Street reporters call a debacle on the Stock Exchange holds first page news position. Then one day a New York City bank with 400,000 depositors must paste a piece of paper in its plate glass window, saying: "Closed by order of the State Bank Examiner." Of the surplus credit rising from the cash deposits of its forgotten 400,000 that bank has loaned too much on things such as afterward turn out to be pyramids—for example, skyscrapers.

Do you remember the old lady with the satchel at the window marked "Savings" in the small local bank? She has a friend in New York City who was one of the 400,000. She gets a letter from this friend, saying a bank these days is no place for one's money. It will be safer, even though without interest, in many places a woman can think of. It may be the bottom of the flour can. So this old lady appears again at the window marked "Savings." She wants all her money out. Then the man in overalls comes; he has heard something to the same effect and he wants all of his money out. These two would not matter to the great American banking system as a whole. But remember, this is one of 25,000 banks, in each one of which a few depositors are asking for their money back, all at one time. This, then, is the beginning of that contraction in all the springs and streams and waters of credit that was spoken of before.

What now takes place is the reverse of multiplication. It is deflation. The banker cannot control it. If he has multiplied credit in the ratio of ten for one, so, as his depositors take away their money, he must reduce credit in the same ratio. That is to say, for each dollar of cash that is taken out of his hands, he must call back from somewhere ten dollars of credit. Thus the vast and sensitive mechanism of credit, running at high speed, is put suddenly in reverse motion, with a frightful clashing of gears.

Return to the case of the little local bank, where you were sitting. As its depositors continue to withdraw cash, it must call in credit. First it sends word by telephone or telegraph to the big New York City bank, saying: "Please return our credit. We need it."

But since the New York bank, remember, has loaned that credit out, it must in turn call it back from some one else. If it has loaned it on the Stock Exchange to brokers, who have loaned it to speculators, these must give it back. But suppose the New York City banks that supply the Stock Exchange with credit are all calling at the same time for it to be returned, because thousands of local banks all over the country, where the credit came from, are calling upon them to return it.

In that case the Stock Exchange brokers are sunk. They cannot replace the credit they are called upon to give up, because the sources of credit are now contracting. This being the fact, the brokers say to their customers, namely, the speculators: "We are sorry and this is awful, but there is no more credit. The banks are calling our loans. We cannot carry your securities any longer on credit. If you cannot pay for them in cash in the next fifteen minutes, we shall have to sell them for what they will bring, to save ourselves."

From this cause there is a new day of panic on the Stock Exchange, a further debacle, with hideous wide headlines in the papers. Panic is advertised. The whirling Stock Exchange pyramid is falling, for want of credit to sustain it. This is an effect that becomes in turn a cause. Because of the headlong decline in prices on the Stock Exchange, in which the loss of imaginary wealth is measured, and for other reasons not exactly given, more banks fail. Each day the lines of anxious depositors grow longer. Thus the waters of credit continue to contract, and the rate is accelerated.

But suppose the New York bank has loaned the credit to a bank in Berlin and cannot get it back at all. What will it do in that case? For it is obliged either to return the credit to the small local bank that is demanding it back or confess itself insolvent. Well, in that case the New York bank must sell some securities out of its own reserve investments. But if all the New York banks are doing the same thing at the same time, as more or less they will be, the effect on the Stock Exchange is even worse. The banks will be selling bonds where speculators would be selling only stocks, and the effect upon the mind of the country from a fall in bonds is much more disturbing.

Now what you are looking at is liquidation. Credit is contracting because these thousands of forgotten bank depositors are calling for their money; and because credit is contracting everybody is calling at once for the return of it to its source, and there is no way for the person who last borrowed to return it but to sell something.

Suppose, however, that the local bank gets its credit back from the New York bank. It is not enough. Its depositors continue to take their money out; more credit must be called in—always, remember, ten for one. Somebody, somewhere, must give up ten dollars of credit for each dollar of actual money the depositors withdraw. The local bank next thinks of selling its South American bonds. That is another way of calling credit back.

Somebody will have to buy the bonds, of course, but that simply means that whoever buys them from the bank will be taking the bank's place as creditor of the South American government that issued the bonds. The bank need not worry about who that buyer is; the transaction will take place in the open bond market, where the law of *caveat emptor* holds. Buyer, beware.

But when the local bank goes to sell its South American bonds it finds them quoted at thirty—the same bonds it paid ninety for. The South American government is in financial trouble, and all the buyers standing in the bond market know it; that is why they will offer only thirty for the bonds. If the bank sells them at thirty it will have lost forever two-thirds of the credit it loaned to the South American government. Besides, if that is all it can get for the bonds, it will not greatly help to sell them. So it puts these bonds aside and looks at its German bonds. But German bonds also have collapsed. Their condition may be as bad, or worse, because Germany is in trouble. What else can the bank sell? It can sell its United States government bonds; yet even in these there is a considerable loss. They have declined in price under the selling of hundreds, thousands, of other banks all in the same dilemma, all tempted to sell their United States government bonds instead of worse bonds on which they cannot affort to take the loss.

Having got back the credit it loaned to the United States government, by selling its United States government bonds, the local bank goes on for a while, paying off its depositors, exhorting them to desist, telling them everything will be all right, hoping for the best. Then one day the bank examiner from the comptroller's office at Washington comes unexpectedly to look at the books and decide if the bank is solvent. Having looked at the books he says: "See here! You have sold all of your best assets. Now to make your books balance with bad assets you still value them at what you paid for them. These foreign bonds, for example—still valued on your books at ninety and ninety-five when you know very well they are worth in the market today only thirty or thirty-five. You are not a solvent bank. You will have to close."

Then the fatal piece of white paper is pasted on the plate glass, and all the depositors then at the windows asking for their money are put out.

That—almost exactly that—happened to 3,635 banks of all

kinds in the two years 1930 and 1931. The deposits of these 3,635 ruined banks were more than $2.5 billion.

It is easily forgotten that the depositor who stands outside to read the bank examiner's verdict through the glass was the original lender.

Consider what it is a depositor does. It is clear enough that when he makes a deposit he is lending money to the bank. But what does the money represent? If it is earned money the depositor brings, it represents something of equal value produced by his own exertions, something he would sooner save than consume. It may be a cord of wood. Suppose it.

There are only a few things to do with a surplus cord of wood. If you store it for you own future use it represents earned leisure. If you exchange it with a neighbor for something else you want that is conversion by crude barter. In neither case is there any increase. It is all the time one cord of wood. You may sell it for money. If you hoard the money you have the equivalent of one cord of wood and yet no increase. But suppose you take the money to the bank and leave it there at interest. In that case you have loaned the bank your surplus labor to the value of a cord of wood, and there is the beginning of increase. Another industrious man, who is without tools, borrows money from the bank to buy an ax, a maul, and some wedges. These tools represent your cord of wood. With these tools that man chops three cords of wood. One he wants for himself and two he sells. With the proceeds of one he returns to the bank the money he borrowed to buy the tools. He has still in his hand the proceeds of the third cord, which is profit or increase. Let him resolve, instead of spending the increase, to save it. He puts it in the bank. Now the bank has two cords of wood where there was but one before—not the cordwood itself, not the labor itself, but the money agent of labor; besides which are the tools still in the man's hand. All this from one surplus cord of wood to begin with.

Thus we accumulate wealth, and there is no limit to it, provided the labor is not lost.

Now suppose a third man comes and borrows all of that money to build a toy in the meaning of a pyramid that has no economic value, or to make an unlucky speculation, or to buy something he is impatient to enjoy before he has produced anything of equivalent value and then afterward fails to produce the equivalent, so that it turns out that he is unable to pay interest or return the principal. We say in that case the money is lost. Really it is not. It still exists. But what the money represented is lost, and that was the amount of labor necessary to produce two cords of wood.

There is neither value nor power in money itself, only in what it represents. Every dollar of actual money should betoken that a dollar's worth of wealth has been somewhere in some form produced; every dollar of credit multiplied upon that money by the banker should signify that somewhere in some form a dollar's worth of wealth is in process of creation.

Anything that happens to money to debase it, to degrade its relation to the total sum of wealth, so as to impair its buying power, is something that happens to people who have loaned their labor to the banks.

Why do we confine the function of money issue to the government, and have very rigid laws concerning the exercise of that function by the government, and make counterfeiting a crime? All that is with the idea of keeping the value of money constant, for if money is permitted to increase faster than the wealth of things which we price in money, then the value of labor saved in the form of money will deteriorate like a cord of wood in the weather. When for any reason a government is moved to embrace legal counterfeiting, when it begins to issue spurious money—money that has no definite relation to any form of wealth in being or in process—the sequel is well known. There is progressive inflation, which, once it begins, there is no stopping or controlling, short of the final disaster. At the end, the savings of a lifetime, reconverted into money, may not be enough to buy a hat.

This we have learned about money itself, dimly. We have yet to learn it about credit, even dimly.

To any suggestion that the government shall set its printing presses free and flood the country with fiat money, all our economic intelligence reacts with no. Only those will say yes who are mentally or politically unsound. And if a government is obliged by vote of the unsound to do it, then everybody, including the unsound, will begin to hoard gold because gold is the one kind of money no government can make or dilute. Or if it were proposed that every bank should have the privilege to issue money as it might think fit, entirely in its own discretion, we should all know better. Even banks would say no to that. It is not only that people cannot trust private bankers with that privilege; private bankers would be unwilling to trust one another with it.

Yet on this jealously guarded base of money itself, banks are free to inflate and multiply credit, each in its own discretion, notwithstanding the fact that the inflation of money and the inflation of credit are similar evils, producing similar miseries. Inflation of credit—ecstasy, delusion, fantastic enrichment. Deflation of credit—depression, crisis, remorse. One state succeeds the other and there is no escape, for one is cause and one is effect.

On Saving Europe
(The Moratorium)

"A little debt makes a debtor, but a great one an enemy."
— GNOMOLOGIA

Take a text from the news as it was printed in the *New York Times* on Monday, June 23, 1931: "Led by New York, tremendous buying enthusiasm swept over the security and commodity markets of the world yesterday in response to week-end developments reflecting the favorable reception of President Hoover's proposal for a one-year moratorium on war debts and reparations. The worldwide advance in prices added billions of dollars to open market values, with stocks, bonds, grain, cotton, sugar, silver and lead in heavy demand. Pronounced strength developed in the German bond list, the gains ranging from 2 to 13½ points.... United States government bonds failed to participate in the move, all of them closing behind minus signs."

The last line fell obscurely at the end of a paragraph. And that was all the notice any one bestowed upon the most significant fact of a delirious day, namely, the fact that everything in the world went up with the single exception of United States government bonds. And why was that? United States government bonds were telling why, and telling it loudly to such as would listen. They were telling it in the language of quotations, and this is what they were saying:

"Again this business of saving Europe with American credit! Do you ever count up what it has cost you already? It is becoming more and more costly; and, besides, you may not be saving Europe at all. You may be only inflating her. Better may turn out to be worse."

As it did. The worldwide rise in everything but United States government bonds was fictitious, a momentary delusion. Worse was to come.

Specifically, the Hoover debt holiday plan was to save Germany from financial collapse and so avert a disaster that had been bound to react in a ghastly manner upon the whole structure of international finance. The first cost to us was reckoned at $250 million. That was the sum we should have to forgo on account of war debts owing by Great Britain, France, Belgium, Italy, and others to the American Treasury. We could not propose simply that Germany should stop paying reparations for a year to her European creditors. That would have cost Great Britain, France, Belgium, Italy, and others too much. They could not afford it. If they had to forgo reparations from Germany and still pay interest to the United States Treasury on their American war debts they would be hurt in their pockets. So what we proposed was that if Germany's European creditors would give her one year of grace on reparations, the United States would give them one year of grace on their war debt payments to the American Treasury.

Even so there were difficulties, because it would still cost Europe herself something to save Germany. The situation was that France, Great Britain, Belgium, and others had been collecting as reparations from Germany a little more than $400 million a year and paying the United States on account of their war debts to the American Treasury a little less than $250 million a year. Thus a general international war debt holiday to save Germany would cost them the difference, or about $150 million. Great Britain had been collecting from her war debtors only $50 million more than she had been paying to the United States on account of her own American war debt; and she was willing. But France had been collecting from Germany $100 million more than she had been paying to the United States Treasury on account of her war debt, and she was unwilling. After long and painful negotiations it was agreed, for the sake of the debt holiday plan and to save Germany, that France should receive special treatment. An irreducible portion of her reparations money would be paid by Germany to the International Bank at Basle and then reloaned by France to

Germany under a new arrangement. Everybody else took Germany's word for it.

Thus the plan took effect. It cost us $250 million. Well, a little more. While Germany's European creditors were debating the plan and higgling over what it was going to cost them, the Federal Reserve Bank in New York made a direct loan to the German Reichsbank to keep it open. Say, then, it had cost us altogether $300 million. Was it not cheap?

We really thought we had done a grand thing; we read every morning in the newspapers that it was a grand thing. The diplomats and chancelleries of Europe were saying so, on typewritten slips, or in interviews, and the American correspondents were quoting them to us by cable. But the typewritten words of diplomats and chancelleries are purposefully suave. What people were really thinking and saying, even the diplomats, was very different. They were saying, among other things: "This is the beginning of the end of our hateful war debts to the U(ncle) S(hylock) Treasury."

Conservative British newspapers did play up to the official Downing Street tune, the more willingly because it happened to be the British season for hating France; all the popular papers were sarcastic.

French opinion was caustic. These Americans, always saying they wouldn't and didn't, now again blundering their hands into the affairs of Europe, not understanding them at all. Interfering without knowing what it was they interfered with. Using their power of credit to dictate terms between France and Germany. Why shouldn't they lend their credit as credit merely, in a financial way, and otherwise mind their own business? Besides, they were in bad manners, as usual, to propose that France should forgo German reparations for a year without having first consulted France about it.

Comment in Germany was brutal and a little exultant. The Americans were obliged to save Germany from bankruptcy in order to protect the $2.5 billion or more they had already loaned to her. It was to save themselves they were saving her and saving Europe.

However, we still thought very well of it ourselves. And in any case, looking at it unromantically, the solvency of Europe was a bargain at $300 million, if really we had saved it. But in a little while it appeared very clearly that we hadn't. Within two weeks the whole of that $300 million credit had been swallowed up and Europe was saying to us:

"Now see what has happened! The Hoover plan was all right; the intention was good. Only it was inadequate in the first place, and then, unfortunately, the dilatory and public discussion of it by the nations concerned has advertised Germany's condition to the whole world. Now all of Germany's private creditors are in a panic. American banks are calling their deposits out of German banks. The Germans themselves are in flight from the mark. What are you going to do about it? If after this you let Germany go down, it had been better to have done nothing at all. And if you let Germany go down, all of Europe may crash."

So there had to be a second Hoover plan to save Europe. The second plan was that American banks should stop calling their deposits and short-term credits out of Germany and relend her the money for a certain period, say, six months. That meant probably $600 million more American credit. The cost of saving Germany was suddenly multiplied by three. Nevertheless, it had to be done, and it was done under the direction of an American banker who was called to Europe for that purpose.

Yet who could say what it was worth to save Germany, first for her own sake and then for the sake of Europe? It was no longer a bargain; still, thinking of the enormous investment of American money in Germany, now all in jeopardy, it might be worth even a billion dollars—that is to say again, provided we had really saved the situation. But had we? No.

In a few days more it was clear that what all this American credit had bought was only a postponement of evil. The German crisis had still to be met in some radical manner, or else what would happen at the end of the Hoover holiday, or, even before that, when the money perforce reloaned by American banks in Germany for six months was due again? The only radical solution Germany can think of, naturally, is to get rid of reparations; then to borrow more American credit. And the only radical solution the rest of Europe can think of is to get their American war debts cancelled.

But there had been hardly time to begin thinking of radical solutions before another crisis developed. There was an international run on the Bank of England for gold. Her gold began to give out. What could the Old Lady of Threadneedle Street do? What could save the credit of the Bank of England? Only American credit could do that. So the Bank of England came to New York and got a big loan from the Federal Reserve Bank.

American credit had twice saved Germany, once for herself and once for the sake of Europe, and now it had saved the Bank of England—all in less than three months. And the cost had been roughly a billion and a quarter.

Who still could say it had not been worth it?

But again the sigh of relief was interrupted. After all that, another crisis. Germany was not saved; she had been only floated on a raft of American credit. Europe as a whole was not saved because Germany wasn't. And for these reasons the Bank of England discovered immediately that the loan it had got from the Federal Reserve Bank in New York was not enough. That is to say, the Bank of England itself was not saved. It had underestimated the amount of saving required. What to do?

Everybody thought of the same thing at once, as if it were new—the same magic, the same miraculous fluid. More American credit.

But now certain new difficulties. One is that the Bank of England cannot borrow enough. Besides, going to New York again so soon with more IOUs in her hand will hurt her credit. The American bankers may lift their eyebrows. The next idea is that the British government itself shall borrow American credit to save the Bank of England. The only weakness of this idea is that the Labor government of Great Britain as it stands is not in good credit. It is a socialist government and year after year it has been closing the national account book in red ink. It spends so much money upon schemes of social benefit, particularly in the form of a public wage to the unemployed, that it cannot balance its budget. How will it look for the British government to go asking for American credit when it is already spending more than its income and cannot balance its budget?

American bankers, indeed, had been sounded out to see if they would mind. They had not lifted their eyebrows, but they had said: "Really, before expecting us to float a British loan you ought to do something about your books. They are too much talked about. Can't you economize, spend somewhat less on these meritorious social schemes and balance your budget? If you did that the talk about the red ink in your national account book would stop and then it would be easy enough to float a British loan in America, or to give the British Treasury any amount of bank credit.''

Whereupon the British decided to change their government, adopt a program of social economy and balance their budget. This had long been indicated as a necessary thing to do. It was the insolvency of the socialist Labor government, among other things, that was hurting the credit of the pound sterling. Nevertheless, the disagreeable task of reducing public expenditures was postponed until the Bank of England had exhausted its power to borrow American credit on its IOUs. Then it became imperative for the British Treasury to put itself in good standing as a borrower.

When the news came from London that the British had changed their government and now were going to balance their budget, Wall Street bankers were already discussing a loan to Great Britain. ''They reiterated their preparedness,'' said the *New York Times*, August 26, ''to provide a substantial loan if the new government requires it.'' Further: ''The amount, bankers said, should be as large as can be readily supplied by the banks of the country and the credit should run at least a year. A number of bankers believe Great Britain would benefit from a long-term loan and a few of them believe British credit is still strong enough to make a public offering possible even in the present depressed bond market.''

The next day the news in Wall Street was that negotiations had been formally opened and on the third day it was announced that American bankers had loaned the British Treasury $200 million for a year.

But what was the popular reaction in England? The Americans had used their power of credit to interfere in the politics of Great Britain, even to the point of demanding the overthrow of the Labor government. That was the reaction. The *Daily Herald*, organ of the Labor party that had been ruling England, said: ''Among the reasons Mr. MacDonald advances for imposing new privations on the most unfortunate section of the nation is the 'pressure of public opinion abroad.' Whose opinion? Not that of the democracies of Europe or America, oppressed by unemployment and distress for similar reasons, but that of foreign bankers, who laid down to the British Government terms, including changes in the unemployment benefit scheme, upon which and alone upon which they were prepared to render financial aid to the Bank of England.'' It said the Federal Reserve Bank of New York had put a pistol to England's head.

Which was to say, the Americans had no right to name the terms on which they would lend their money to save the Bank of England or to save the credit of the British Treasury. They ought to lend their money and mind their own business.

How do people arrive at this ground of unreason—the English people, who before us were the world's principal creditors with a creditor mentality?

It is not simply that political passions have distorted the facts. That is true. But the facts belong to finance and finance is lost in its own world. It knows neither the way to go on nor how to go back. Having raised international debt to a new order of magnitude, now it faces international insolvency of the same grand order, and it is appalled. It cannot manage the facts. The only solution it can think of is more European debt, more American credit. By itself it cannot create any more debt. If the resources of private credit are not quite exhausted, the credulity of the creditor is about to be. But there may be still some resource left in the public credit of Europe. Finance at this point adopts the mentality of the crowd in the street. Let government do it. Let all the European governments increase their debts who can, to save themselves and one another. This is literal.

By agency of international finance, Germany, in six or seven years, borrowed nearly $4 billion, two-thirds of it from American lenders. It was much more than Germany could afford to borrow—that is, if she cared anything at all about her own solvency. Having procured this money to be loaned to Germany, having exhausted every kind of German security that could be made to look like a bond, international finance came to the sequel and said: "Germany must have more credit, for else her whole financial structure will collapse, and if that happens international finance cannot answer for the consequences. They will be terrible. But Germany has no more security to offer. Therefore international finance cannot float another German loan. But if Germany's creditors will collectively guarantee a German bond issue, international finance can float that.''

Try going on from there. Suppose Germany's European creditors, namely, Great Britain, France, Italy, Belgium, and others should guarantee a German bond issued for more American credit. When that credit was exhausted, what would happen? Perhaps then, in order to go on lending American credit to Europe, we should have to guarantee our own loans. And what better security could you ask? An American loan to Europe guaranteed by Americans!

Well, and what is so very strange about that idea? All the American war loans and all the American postarmistice loans to Europe were guaranteed by the United States government. It borrowed the money on Liberty Bonds and guaranteed them. If Europe does not pay this debt the American government will. It cannot be wiped out or cancelled or reduced. It can only be transferred from the European taxpayer to the American taxpayer.

If the American lender is not a menace to the financial sanity of the Old World, the least definition of him would be to say he is to Europe a fabulous enigma.

Critical European economists say we are the worst lenders in the world, because we lend impulsively, in a reckless, emotional manner, not systematically. That is true. It is true that as lenders, simply so regarded, we are incomprehensible to ourselves and to others. Beyond all considerations of an economic or financial character there is pressing upon us continually that strange sense of obligation to save Europe.

It seized us deeply during the war. It carried us into the war. We were going to save Europe from Germany, the German people from the Hohenzollerns, little nations from big ones, all the people of Europe from the curse of war forever. There were other motives, to be sure. We had money on the side of the Allies, though by such measures as we now use it was very little. Our sympathies went to the Allies. We hated the way Germans made war. Some of us may have been a little afraid of a German Europe. Allied propaganda to get us in had its great effect. Yet for all of this we should never have gone in without the emotional thought images that made a crusade of it.

A war to end war. Where? In Europe. A war to make the world safe for democracy. Where was democracy supposed to be in danger? In Europe. A war to liberate oppressed nationalities. Where?

In Europe. Not a war against the Germans—we said we had no quarrel with the German people—but a war to deliver them from the tyranny of their own bad warlords. And from no realistic point of view was any of this our business.

The allied nations were not interested in our thought images, or, if at all, in one only because it worried them, and that was the one about saving the weak from the strong, otherwise, the right of self-determination for little people. The Allies did not care what our reasons were. We could be as romantic as we liked, only so we came in on their side, for unless we did the war was lost. They were not themselves fighting to make the world safe for democracy, nor to end war forever, nor to deliver the German people, nor to put destiny into the hands of little people; they were fighting to beat Germany, and with American assistance they did beat her. None of the things we thought we were fighting for came out. What survived was a continuing sense of obligation to save Europe.

Our own exertions in a war we had been much better off to stay out of cost us $25 billion. Then, in addition to that, we loaned out of the United States Treasury more than $10 billion to our own associates. Lending to Europe out of the United States Treasury ended with the postarmistice loans. Then private lending began—lending by American banks and American investors. Counting our own direct war expenditures, the war loans, the postarmistice loans, and then the private lending since, Europe has cost us more than $40 billion in less than fifteen years. That sum would have represented one-fifth of our total national wealth in the year 1914.

Cast out the cost of our own war exertions. Pass the war loans by the United States Treasury to the Allies out of the proceeds of Liberty Bonds. Say that under the circumstances we were morally obliged to make them, whether anything should ever come back or not. Pass also the postarmistice loans out of the United States Treasury, which were for cleaning up the wreck in Europe. These constitute the war debts for which now we are hated in Europe and which no doubt will turn out to be worth very little. If the United States Treasury went to Wall Street to sell the long-term bonds it took from the Allies in place of their promissory notes, it would be lucky to get twenty cents on the dollar for them.

So consider only the private debt—that is, the American credit delivered to Europe since the war by American banks and American investors. All the terms were financial. The character of finance is selfish. Therefore, as to this private debt, representing $5 or $6 billion in American credit poured into Europe during the last eight years, it is permitted to ask: What have we gained thereby?

Definitely, in the first place, not the friendship or good will of Europe. On the contrary, we have raised against ourselves in Europe an ugly debtor mentality. This, you may say, is inevitable in the shape of human nature; creditors must expect it and allow for it. But what makes it much worse in Europe and gives it a sinister political importance is the prejudiced manner in which it is exploited, not only by the press and the politicians, but by responsible statesmen, by finance ministers who cannot balance their budgets, by governments when it is necessary to increase taxes.

Germany tells her people that if they did not have to pay reparations—called tribute—to the once allied nations, German wages would go up, German taxes would come down, German poverty would vanish, the German sun would rise.

The once allied nations say to Germany they are sorry; if they did not have to pay their war debts to the United States Treasury they could forgo reparations, or in any case a great part of them, perhaps as much as two-thirds. Yet all the time they keep saying to their own people that their troubles are multiplied upon them by the necessity to remit enormous sums each year to the United States Treasury on account of their war debts. That they collect these sums first from Germany as reparations is not emphasized. And the fact that so far there has been no payment of either reparations or war debts but with the aid of American credit does not interest them at all.

American loans to Germany have enabled her to pay reparations. Out of reparations from Germany the others make their annual payments on their war debts to the American government. Anything we have yet got back from Europe was our own money, the worse for wear, and very little of that. But if you say this to a European, even to one who knows, he is offended. Very few of them do know, as a matter of fact; it is easier to believe what they hear from those who exploit the debtor mentality.

For a long time it was supposed that European feeling against America as the Shylock nation was owing to the nature of the debt

—that it was a war debt and had a public character. Certainly there would be no such unreasonable feeling against a debt owing to private creditors. So we said, and saying it we continued to lend American credit in Europe until the weight of the private debt exceeded that of the war debt. Owing to its sheer magnitude this private debt now begins to assume a public character, and as it does there begins to rise about it and against it the same excitable popular feeling. Why are Americans so rich? Where do they get all this credit? Do they mean to enslave the world with their gold?

This is the sequel international finance does not foresee. When it comes suddenly to the end of its own resources, as it did in 1931, it must call on governments to interfere; after that all talk of keeping finance free of politics is sheer nonsense.

The real crisis in Germany last summer came after all nations had been relieved of war debts for one year, under the first Hoover plan. It was concerning the solvency of Germany in respect of her debt to private creditors that a seven-power conference of prime ministers was held in London in July. There the United States was represented by the American secretary of state and the American secretary of the treasury, and there came forth the second Hoover plan, to save Germany from having to default on her debt, not to other governments, but to private creditors. The situation had got beyond the control of international finance; therefore, governments were obliged to interfere.

Again, later, when the British had to change their government in order to borrow American credit to save the Bank of England, a financial transaction with private creditors assumed a public character. The British government borrowed the money, not from the American government, but from American bankers. Nevertheless, because the American bankers had stipulated for public expenditures to be reduced in England and for the British budget to be balanced, it was possible, even plausible, for the British Labor party to say the Americans had exerted their colossal money power to destroy the Labor government of Great Britain; and there are hundreds of thousands of unemployed in England who will think American bankers responsible for their diminished weekly dole out of the British public funds.

A private international debt is easily defined; it represents borrowing by private persons in one country from private persons in another. So also is a public international debt easily defined; it is a debt owed by one government to another. But debt may be private on one side and public on the other, as when the government of one nation borrows from private lenders in another. But let it be strictly a private debt, owing by the nationals of one country to the nationals of another, and yet if it becomes so large as to endanger the solvency and economic freedom of the debtor people, or so large as to alter their economic relations adversely, it will clothe itself with a public character and political consequences are bound to follow.

Our loans to Europe are of all kinds. They represent borrowing by European governments from the American government, they represent borrowing by private persons and private organizations in Europe from private American lenders, and they represent borrowing by European governments and states and municipalities from private American creditors. Less and less do these distinctions matter, because more and more the character of an American loan is merely that particular aspect of one great body of debt. The political implications of it simply as debt take us unawares.

In the September 1931 number of the *Revue des Deux Mondes,* M. Henri Bérenger, formerly French ambassador to the United States and coauthor of the Mellon-Bérenger war-debt funding agreement between France and the American government, has an essay in the fine style of French logic on what has happened to the foreign policy of these Americans. For 145 years they had founded their foreign policy on Washington's farewell address to the American Congress. The words were few. No foreign entanglements. Woodrow Wilson was the first president to preach another doctrine, and the Americans rejected both him and his doctrine, and thereafter they sent only official observers to sit in the councils of Europe. "Then," says M. Bérenger, "President Hoover issues his messages to the world and sends his Secretary of the Treasury and his Secretary of State to negotiate with European ministers. This came after the launching of the presidential message of June 20, which to all intents and purposes was a message of entanglement. What has taken place on the other side of the Atlantic to make such derogation of the Washington doctrine possible, even popular?"

He answers his own question, saying: "For seven years American bankers have been engaged in entangling the United States with Europe.... Indeed, the network of steel and gold that America has cast upon Europe has been so powerful that it has become jammed of its own weight. A crash in Berlin is immediately felt in Washington and every panic in Frankfort causes trembling in Wall Street. When the crisis becomes worse and extends itself to the City of London the United States is so entangled that it is in danger of being strangled."

The French see it. In less than ten years finance has accomplished a fact the idea of which had been rejected by the American people for a century and a half, namely, the fact of foreign entanglement.

Since our lending to Europe bears us no friendship, only more and more dislike, and since it has caught us in a net of foreign entanglements contrary to our native wisdom, the question returns unanswered. What do we get out of it?

Now the voice of foreign commerce, saying: "But our lending abroad did increase our export trade. Our loans to Europe enabled her to buy from us great quantities of goods that otherwise she had been unable to buy. This kept our factories going, it kept our own labor employed." And it is so, it did for a while. There is probably no point beyond which your export trade cannot be still further inflated so long as you lend people the money with which to buy your goods. But if it is good business when, having loaned your foreign customers the money to buy with, the goods are no sooner gone than you begin to wonder if you will get anything back, unless again you lend them the money to pay you with or forgive what they already owe—if that is business at all, then common sense is daftness and international finance has in itself the secret of wisdom.

Another voice is heard, saying: "But remember, this modern world is all one place. No nation may enjoy separate prosperity, not even this one. A war-haggard Europe was properly the concern of a country that had resources to spare.... That was reason enough for putting American credit at the command of Europe. Besides that it was our duty to do it, we should have been intelligent to do it on the ground of enlightened selfishness."

This high and excellent thought belongs to a harmony the world is not ready to play. There is first the probability that it will be embraced from opposite sides differently, by the lenders with one enthusiasm and by the borrowers with another, and that the transactions between them will not be governed by the simple rules of prudence, judgment, and moral responsibility. When, moreover, you talk of lending as a duty, what do you mean? And how afterward shall you treat the contract? There is the further danger that the thought will be degraded to the saying that a rich nation, only because it is richer than others, is obliged to disperse its surplus among the envious and less fortunate. That idea, indeed, has been asserted by many European doctors of political economy, who either do not see or care not that international borrowing tends thereby to become reckless and irresponsible, and is soon tinged with the ancient thought of plunder.

The Rescue of Germany
(The Great August Crisis)

The war has lasted sixteen years.
German guilt was a lie.
The Treaty of Versailles is the great crime of modern history.
Reparations are tribute.
In 1917 America joined the Allies against Germany because then her money was on that side.
Among nations, the debtor is dear to the creditor.
The Hoover debt holiday plan in 1931 was to protect two billion in American money in Germany, for now America is bound by what Germany owes her to be Germany's political friend.
    — SELECTIONS FROM CURRENT GERMAN SAYINGS

Again, for the third time, Germany was threatening to sink in the sea of insolvency with all her creditors on board; again it was the creditors who frantically worked at the pumps. Their anxiety was greater than Germany's own. Why? For the singular reason that in this sea only creditors can drown.

If Germany sinks she will rise again, lightened by the loss of her creditors. Twice the creditors, unable otherwise to keep her afloat, have cast overboard great parcels of debt, and that at first was easy to do because the debt was political. The name of it was reparations. But now, in this third crisis, there are two kinds of debt and two kinds of creditors on board, all in the same dilemma. There is what survives of the original reparations debt, and there is now, besides, an enormous private debt, owing not by the German government to other governments, but owing by the German government, by all the German states, by German municipalities, by German banks, by German industry, to private lenders all over the world. This is new debt, created in the last six or seven years. The amount of it is nearly $4 billion. Roughly two-thirds of it is owing to American banks, American investors, American lenders.

One value of this great private debt to Germany is that she can play it against the political debt.

As she watches her creditors working at the pumps she keeps saying: "Throw over the rest of the reparations debt. That is what is sinking us. Cast that away and the rest will float."

Then to her private creditors alone she says: "Don't you see how you can save yourselves? Only side with us and we will get rid of the reparations debt entirely. We tell you the rest will float."

This suggestion tends to divide the creditors and they begin quarreling among themselves. But they cannot be sure that if the reparations debt be jettisoned the rest will float. They are not sure of anything about Germany. So, in frustration, they appoint an international committee of experts to examine the ship from both the German point of view and that of the creditors, to reconcile them, and to say what burden of debt the ship can afford to bear, Germany willing.

The first international committee of experts had to work in a diving bell. Germany then, in 1924, was totally submerged. By inflating her money until it was worthless she had committed an act of complete national insolvency, internal and external. Nothing like it had ever happened before. Nevertheless, the experts found the ship itself to be quite sound and so reported. All that was necessary was to float it again on a tide of confidence. Once afloat it could bear a reparations debt burden of $625 million a year.

That was the Dawes Plan; and on the undertaking to make it work the German government borrowed $200 million in gold from Great Britain, France, and the United States, to begin a policy of fulfillment. Then immediately Germany at large launched herself upon a career of borrowing so amazing and reckless as to correspond to nothing that had ever happened before in the history of international finance, except, by contrast, her preceding career in bankruptcy by inflation. And this was the beginning of the private debt.

Five years later the Dawes Plan was sinking the ship. The sum of $625 million a year was a disastrous thing in itself; but what made it very much worse was that the Dawes Plan did not say for how many years this burden should be carried. It had not fixed the total amount of reparations to be paid, only the annual payment on account. Unless the creditors would agree to fix a total, so that Germany might at least see the end of reparations, there was nothing for her to do but to embrace despair and sink again.

Then a second committee of international experts made an analysis of her resources and said she could afford to pay only $400 million a year. That was the Young Plan; and on the undertaking to make that plan work, the German government borrowed $300 million from Great Britain, France, and the United States, to launch a second policy of fulfillment.

But before the Young Plan had begun to work, the former head of the German Reichsbank and other Germans were going up and down in the world proclaiming the authentic propaganda that reparations still were bringing Germany to ruin; that unless she was relieved of that burden she would surely sink, and that if a second act of national insolvency, such as preceded the Dawes Plan, was the only way of escape, then this, with all its terrors, might come to seem the lesser German sacrifice.

It is weird to remember that with this propaganda running higher and higher, still Germany could continue to borrow abroad on a scale hitherto unheard of. American investors went on buying German bonds because the rate of interest was high; American banks went on putting their surplus funds on deposit in German banks for the same reason. They all said: "Oh, that is political propaganda about reparations. It has nothing to do with private finance or private investments." Nobody could imagine that the Germans would attack their own credit and really mean it; or that a second act of national bankruptcy was possible. It was a little like the warning on the sinking of the *Lusitania.* There it was, cold and authentic, and nobody believed it.

Suddenly in June 1931 the lesser sacrifice did nevertheless become imminent. Germany was at the brink of national insolvency and calling on her creditors to forbear and save her from that disaster. Her inflated financial structure was about to fall.

The Reichsbank was about to shut up. In that case, naturally, she would be obliged to default on the whole of her foreign debt, both political and private, and the private debt, owing not to governments but to foreign investors and foreign banks, had reached the prodigious total of nearly $4 billion. Could international finance afford to let such a thing happen? Were not Germany's creditors obliged in their own interest to come to her rescue?

The most sympathetic of Germany's creditors was Great Britain, not because she had more to lose than any other country—she had much less in jeopardy than the United States—but for other and complicated reasons. Every day in June the head of the Bank of England had New York on the telephone to tell American bankers how desperate the German situation was, how daily it grew worse, and why it behooved the United States to take great measures. Only the United States had the resources to save Germany. England alone was helpless to avert the calamity. France was obscure. The United States was obliged in its own interest to act. For suppose Germany failed. What would happen to American banks with enormous sums on deposit in German banks? And what would happen to the German bonds that had been sold to banks and private investors all over the United States? What would happen to American banks that had those German bonds in their investment reserves? When the head of the Bank of England was not calling New York, the British government itself was calling Washington and saying the same things.

Such were the circumstances under which President Hoover proposed an international debt holiday. No reparations to be collected by the former Allies from Germany, no payments to be made by Europe on account of war debts to the United States Treasury, for a period of one year. The effect of this was a loan of $400 million to Germany. That was the amount she would have had otherwise to pay away on account of reparations. And besides that effect, international finance at the same time made a direct loan of $100 million to the German Reichsbank to meet any emergency. The money was provided by the Federal Reserve Bank of New York, the Bank of England, and the Bank of France. On this day's work international finance heaved a great sigh. Nothing less than the bankruptcy of Germany had been averted. For several days there was a wonderful rise in German bonds, in securities of all kinds, even in commodities, the whole world over.

What followed immediately was a headlong flight from the German mark. Private banks in England, France, Holland, Switzerland, and the United States that had been keeping money in German banks because the rate of interest was high were, on second thought, more anxious than ever to call their deposits home, for after all, a year was a short time and nobody knew what would happen at the end of the holiday.

But that was not all. The Germans themselves were in flight from the mark. They had been stealing away from it quietly for a year or more; now they began to run. They took German marks to the Reichsbank and bought dollars in New York, pounds sterling in London, French francs in Paris. This could be done through the mechanism of foreign exchange; and when they had exchanged their marks at the Reichsbank for dollars payable in New York, pounds sterling payable in London, and French francs payable in Paris, they had then only to wire to New York, to London, and to Paris to keep their dollars, their pounds sterling, and their francs on deposit. Germans who knew not how to convert German marks into foreign bank deposits through the mechanism of foreign exchange found simple ways to get rid of them. For example, they would go to the nearest border and tender the largest possible German mark bill for a small railroad ticket, wanting not the little journey into a foreign country but the change in Dutch guilders or Swiss francs, for hoarding.

The Hoover debt holiday plan took effect on June 30, and Germany on that date, with $400 million less to pay out and $100 million new credit borrowed at the same time, was half a billion dollars to the good. Nevertheless, within ten days Dr. Luther, head of the German Reichsbank, was going about Europe in an airplane, to Basle, to Paris, to London, saying Germany must have immediately the loan of half a billion dollars more. The whole benefit of the Hoover debt holiday plan had been swallowed up in the flight from the German mark, and Germany's financial plight was much worse than before. The lesser German sacrifice, that is to say, the bankruptcy of Germany, now was really imminent.

International finance was horrified. Where was the end of this? The Germans rushing their own money out of Germany and Germany at the same time imploring her creditors to put more in, to save her and to save themselves!

"It is a sieve," said the French. "A perfect sieve. Moreover, it is very probably a trap. Does Germany think that by threatening to repudiate her debts she can oblige her creditors to go on putting more and more in, merely in order to get a fixed amount out?"

The French were in a very strong position—much stronger than the English. The Bank of England had been steadily losing gold for a long time and was greatly worried about it, whereas the Bank of France had the second largest gold fund in the world and was steadily increasing it. The French knew very well that the idea of another great international loan to Germany would fail if they declined to support it. So they said: "Very well. We will consider taking part in another international loan to Germany provided the Germans will behave as debtors should. Debtors ought not to be cultivating a military spirit toward their creditors. Therefore, let the Germans disband their Steel Helmets, which represent the old military spirit again. Let them stop spending their creditors' money for what they call pocket battleships, which are really very formidable sea weapons. Let them undo their bargain of union with Austria, which is contrary to the Treaty of Versailles."

At this Dr. Luther flew home to Berlin. He represented only the German Reichsbank, and nothing else of the German government; he was therefore not competent to discuss political matters.

On his return a song of bitterness burst in Germany. The war still! The French again! They would take advantage of Germany's desperate necessities to make humiliating political demands. Having ruined the Hoover plan by making difficulties about it until the grand effect was lost, now they would use their financial strength to force Germany into economic slavery.

The English, dreading more than any other nation a crash of the financial structure of Europe, spilled unction on these waters. They proposed a conference of prime ministers to be held in London and persuaded the German chancellor to come by way of Paris and stop there in his best German manner for such impression as it might make on the implacable French nature. The German chancellor did, taking with him his foreign minister and a body of eminent experts. The French received them at the railway station under an arch of flowers. Any one who even a little understands the French would know what that meant. It meant that the French were in a logical mood and that when the embracings were over they would find themselves astronomically removed from any point of view but their own. And so it was.

Yet what the Germans were saying was enough to make the blood of international finance run cold. They were saying that Germany had no plan of her own to propose. She had only the facts to present. It was up to her creditors to regard the facts and then decide whether to save Germany in order to save themselves. The Germans said they were talking not only of their political debt, that is to say, reparations, on account of which they were obliged to find $400 million a year; they were thinking even more of Germany's new private debt, amounting now to nearly $4 billion. This was money Germany and her nationals had borrowed during six years on their bonds and notes and short-dated IOUs from banks and from private investors in America, England, France, Holland, Switzerland, Scandinavia, and elsewhere, and more from Americans than from any of the others. A great deal of it had been what is called short-term credit, that is to say, loans for short periods such as may be renewed again and again if the sky stays blue and yet such as may be suddenly called away at the first sign of bad weather. It had been dangerous to borrow so much short-term credit. They said they knew that all the time. Much of this short-term credit has been unwisely, some of it extravagantly, spent; they knew that also. Admitted it as a fact. Nevertheless, it was necessary to face the facts. Now many of those who had been lending Germany this money were calling for it back. But having spent it, how could Germany give it back, or, in any case, all at once? It was due and payable—yes. The creditors were within their rights to call for it back. But they were calling to the vast deep of ten thousand empty German tills. If they insisted, there was only one thing for Germany to do. That was to confess herself bankrupt and so treat all creditors alike. It was not Germany's problem, really. It was a problem for international finance to solve. The only way for the creditors to get interest or principal out of Germany, or reparations either, was to go on lending her the money to pay them.

At this point of the German discourse international finance began to shudder. For six years it had been pouring money into the German treasury, into German industry, into German banks, saying all the time: "If the world expects Germany to pay reparations it must lend her enormous sums of capital to build up her internal economy." Now Germany saying to her creditors: "If you expect to be paid you must lend us the money to pay you with. To save your investments you must save Germany first."

And what is it Germany must be saved from? First and always from reparations.

But the Germans were not through. They went on to say that unless international finance came to Germany's rescue with an enormous new loan it might expect, first, a total eclipse of German solvency toward the ouside world. After that, what? After that, communism—a red Germany, for what that would mean to the peace and comfort of her neighbors. And suppose this did not happen. Suppose for her own sake she could avoid going red in a political sense. Nevertheless, if now it becomes necessary for Germany to save herself with no more benefit of credit, she will be obliged to go red in an economic sense. She knows how to save herself. She has only to forget her creditors, forget the rules of capital, forget the arrangements by means of which international finance has been trying to support a high capital structure, and simply flood the markets of the world with unlimited quantities of cheap German goods.

So that was what the conference of prime ministers had to face in London.

First, in the obvious aspect, a sinking Germany—sinking for want of an international loan to keep herself afloat. An international loan would be normally the business of international bankers on its merits. But international finance at this time was practically unconscious. Germany had created a situation quite beyond its resources, its experience, or its imagination. International finance is not a bank, not a gold hoard; it is a mechanism. It would be willing enough to take German bonds for half a billion more—if the bonds could be sold. But where could any more German bonds be sold? The world was already full of them, all selling at a terrible discount, because so many holders were trying to get rid of them. International finance, in short, was out of ideas. Possibly the prime ministers with all their heads together could think of something. Anyhow, that was the only hope; that was what the conference was for.

The conference took place in London in the third week of July. The seven principal powers of the world were represented. Six of them were anxious creditors; the seventh was the astonishing debtor. The United States was represented by Mr. Stimson, secretary of state, and by Mr. Mellon, secretary of the treasury.

Regard it. In weight and size and shape it is the most august meeting of high statesmen since wartime. Imagine the opening, the formal gestures, a speech by the British premier saying now every one must forget his own and think only of the whole, of what will be best to do for the good of the world, since only by unselfish international collaboration can they hope to solve the problem before them.

Suppose Germany shall speak next. Has she any plan of her own to propose?

No. Germany is helpless. She has no plan. She submits the facts and leaves the solution to her creditors. All she can think of is that an international loan of half a billion dollars will keep her afloat.

For how long?

That she cannot say. For a while at least. It would mean a breathing space.

What has Germany to offer for such a loan?

Nothing. Germany is helpless. She has nothing left to offer.

But what security?

None, except her promise to pay.

But her promises to pay already exceed her power of performance. Is not that the very problem?

That, of course, is the problem. The Germans admit it simply.

Will Germany be willing to secure such a loan by a lien on her customs receipts, as the French have suggested?

No.

Why not?

Because the German people will not submit to that humiliation. They will destroy any government that dares to propose it.

Will Germany make any political concessions to appease the French, such as to stop building battleships and to disband the troublesome Steel Helmets?

No.

Why not?

Again, because the German people will not suffer that humiliation. They would sooner go red.

But perhaps Germany will agree to stop working for a revision of the treaties? Perhaps she will agree, when this crisis is over, to return to the Young Plan and observe it faithfully, instead of trying meantime to get it revised?

Certainly not. Germany would tactfully remind her very distinguished collaborators that what they are dealing with is a financial crisis. It is a mistake, not to say a breach of concord, to load it with political difficulties.

Very well. But with nothing to yield, nothing to give, nothing to offer that has not already been twice exhausted, on what ground does Germany expect her creditors to lend her another half billion dollars?

The answer is ready. Germany would think her creditors could see the importance of doing it on the ground of their own interest. Suppose they refuse. Suppose they let Germany go. In the first place, the financial consequences will be uncontrollable. They cannot be confined to Germany alone. Germany might have to sink, but her creditors would sink with her, and the effect might well be a worldwide financial crash. Secondly, that would be the end of responsible government in Germany. Suppose then nationalism were to rise in its extreme form, or else communism. In any case Germany would be obliged to save herself, even though to do so it were necessary to repudiate not only her debts but all other forms of economic restraint, cut wages, cut prices, and overwhelm the markets of the world with German goods.

Helpless Germany! Able to challenge her creditors. Able to threaten the political structure of Europe. Able to threaten the economic structure of the world. How had she arrived at this oblique eminence? By intending her mind to it? By taking advantage of the stupidity of the world? By drift of forces that happened to be working for her? And was threaten the right word? No member of the London conference, gazing at the Germans, could answer even the last of these questions.

The English were deeply agitated at the thought of Germany going economically red, much more than at the thought of political bolshevism. A royal commission had just produced a mighty treatise on the necessity to restore the world's price level. Its conclusion was that to stabilize prices at the fallen level would be a calamity. Prices at whatever cost or risk, even if necessary by a process of scientific international inflation, must be stabilized on a higher level, or else a great deal of the world's capital representing what formerly had been a normal expectation of profit, would be forever lost. Dumping, therefore—the thought or word of it—filled the British mind with dismay. Russian dumping was terror enough. A campaign of propaganda to bar Russian goods from English markets was at that moment running in the London press. But how much more formidable would Germany be in that red economic role, with her skill, her experience, her long ambition to dominate the foreign markets of the world, and her powerful industrial machine—the most powerful and efficient in Europe! And how politely the Germans were saying it!

Yet there was no misunderstanding what they meant; moreover, the idea was rising in Germany. The German newspapers were saying that an economic policy of self-saving, with no further benefit of international finance, would have the advantage to "loosen political and financial bonds which were not unconditionally necessary and have hitherto acted only as brakes on our development." And saying this at a time when the German government held the German press in strict censorship.

The English could imagine those mountains of coal visible at the German pit heads breaking over Europe and running down into Italy, to the ruin of the British coal trade; they could see German manufactures underselling British goods everywhere in foreign markets. The British press touched the subject in a very guarded manner, hardly at all. But the *London Times* said it was understood that Mr. Ramsay MacDonald had taken the Germans aside and said to them that a policy of German dumping would bring them into conflict with England. He said England would retaliate, perhaps with no idea whatever in his head of how really it could.

Well, the mighty seven-power conference of six anxious creditors and one astonishing debtor failed to find a magic chemistry. It labored and brought forth two suggestions, then adjourned, pronouncing its own benediction. The suggestions were these: First, that since a new international loan to Germany was not immediately feasible, each of the six creditor governments should recommend to its bankers to leave in Germany the remainder of their deposits instead of calling them home. Second, that a third committee of international experts be called up to study Germany's situation, analyze her necessities, and report.

It sounds very little. From the creditors' point of view it was less than nothing. And yet Germany, with nothing to yield, nothing to give, nothing to offer, had won three major points.

First, she got her loan, though it was involuntary on the part of the lenders. When the principal American and English banks, together with such others as could be bullied or persuaded, agreed to leave their overdue deposits and short-term credits in the German banks, instead of calling them home, that was the equivalent of a loan of more than three-quarters of a billion dollars to Germany. She had the money; she could continue to use it. It had simply been reloaned to her.

Secondly, Germany gained a third international committee of experts to protect her from her creditors; and the American member of this committee was Albert H. Wiggin, head of the Chase National Bank in New York, publicly committed to the proposition that reparations and war debts should be heavily scaled down or cancelled altogether, and that at the same time American tariffs should be reduced in order that Europe might sell more of its goods in American markets.

Thirdly, what Germany most wanted was to hand a mourning wreath upside down on the Young Plan, and that she did.

What the third international committee of experts represented was perhaps the last decline of the make-believe that there could ever be an economic approach to the problem of German reparations. How can there be, when the German government itself officially speaks of reparations as tribute? People who believe reparations are tribute—and the Germans do deeply believe it—will not behave as if reparations were debt. Yet that is how the world has been expecting the Germans to behave. Nor can there be any purely economic solutions with Germany, private or other, so long as Germans keep thinking, "This is the sixteenth—" or, "This is the seventeenth year of the war." Her principal creditors, remember, were her enemies in the war.

It is easy enough to make an economic analysis of the 1931 financial crisis in Germany. That can be done in one sentence. The great German machine, having been raised on borrowed capital to be the most powerful and the most efficient in Europe, was running on borrowed gas. Given that fact, any one would know what the consequences were bound to be. But what is the fact worth? Why was the German machine running on borrowed gas? Why were the Germans putting their own gas out of Germany for safekeeping into the banks of foreign countries, and borrowing gas, that is to say, short-term credit, from other people? Why?

When in early July the head of the German Reichsbank was go-ing about Europe in an airplane, soliciting an international loan of half a billion dollars (gas) to keep the German machine from stalling, to save Germany from bankruptcy—at that time the Ger-mans' own estimate of the amount of German money (gas again) on deposit in New York, London, Paris, Amsterdam, and other foreign money centers was a billion dollars. There was so much German money on deposit in Paris alone that if it had been called for all in one day the French money market would have been demoralized. There was no danger of its being called for. The Germans did not want their own money; they wanted other peo-ple's money.

These you may state as economic facts, bearing on the German crisis. They explain the crisis. Yet they are not themselves to be ex-plained in economic terms. If the Germans had kept their own money at home there need not have been a financial crisis. They had enough gas of their own to keep their machine going. But they preferred to hoard their own in foreign countries. Seeing all this clearly, the French were unable to take a strictly financial view of the German crisis. They kept asking: "Why have the Ger-mans brought this condition upon themselves?" Certainly not for economic reasons.

And remember that all this time the reparations debt has been not an economic burden, not a financial burden, but a mental burden only. Actual burden it never was, for the simple reason that never yet has Germany paid any reparations. She has made the world pay them for her; she has made her creditors pay themselves.

In the beginning she had resorted to the naive expedient of simply printing paper marks and selling them all over the world so long as anybody would buy them. And people did buy them in prodigious quantities. The lower they fell the more they bought, saying all the time, "Germany will never repudiate her money; it is unimaginable," and thinking, therefore, it was a fine specula-tion to buy marks. The buyers of these marks, which were going to be repudiated, and the holders of German bonds receiving in-terest in those same marks—they paid the first reparations, not Germany. Germany took their money in exchange for her paper marks and handed it over to her creditors. When at last the cost of printing and shipping paper marks in bundles was more than the marks would bring, Germany stopped her printing presses, stopped paying reparations, and announced her total insolvency.

Then the French conceived the grim idea of collecting reparations by force. That was when they went into the Ruhr and seized the very heart of Germany's industrial machine. All they proved was that you cannot collect reparations from an unwilling people by force. The Germans would not work their machine to produce tribute for the French. There were strikes and riots and, worse still, threat of wrecking the machine itself or jamming it by sabotage. Imagine it, when the slip of a monkey wrench in the hands of a sullen German workman might cost the French a million francs of tribute. That was the French problem in the Ruhr, where they had the industrial heart of Germany in their hands. Suppose they had said: "Very well, we shall take the machine into our own hands and run it." But that would mean bringing workers and technicians from their own country. There would be no profit in that. Besides, if they did it, they would have a starving, idle German population on their hands. The Ruhr party cost the French more than they got out of it. No reparations that way.

At this impasse the nations of Europe joined to call on the United States, saying: "We are emotionally and politically mad. We have only sanity enough left among us to know that we are. Simply, we cannot think economically. You over there have the vision of distance. Think of a way in which we may go on here in Europe. For unless you can we shall go to pieces. Bring us a plan." We did. We sent them American experts to straighten them out; we gave them the Dawes Plan. Germany accepted it, crossed her heart for a policy of fulfillment, and borrowed $200 million gold to get started with.

Since the Dawes Plan took effect—since 1924, that is to say—Germany's net payments on account of reparations, according to her own figures, have amounted to $2.35 billion.

In the same time, still according to her own statistics, she has borrowed from other countries the incredible sum of $3.75 billion.

This is to say, that since 1924 she has borrowed $1.4 billion more than she has paid out on account of reparations.

Roughly two-thirds of this borrowed money came from the United States. The next largest part of it came from Great Britain.

The rest of it from France, Holland, Switzerland, and other lending countries. More than three-quarters of the total came from her former enemies.

Simply to say that Germany borrowed with one hand and paid reparations with the other, or that out of every dollar she borrowed she paid sixty-three cents in reparations and kept thirty-seven, does not tell the whole story. The money had a circular movement. It went one way into Germany, stopped there for ninety days, six months, a year or more, to work, and then went out another way, like water turning a mill wheel. It is important to remember this, for it explains many otherwise incomprehensible effects. The money did not just go in and out again; it was detained and put to work. That is what people who talk economics mean when they say that with borrowed money Germany built up her internal economy in order to be able to pay reparations and then paid them out of the increase of her wealth. She did build up her internal economy amazingly. She knew how to bend that stream of money on the wheel. And that is how it happens that she is today the second most powerful industrial nation in the world. The United States is first in the world. Germany is first in Europe.

She spent the borrowed money under three heads, namely: *one,* for housing of all kinds; *two,* on her industrial machine, to rebuild it, rationalize it, increase its power; and, *three,* for public works such as parks, baths, civic and recreation centers, schools, stadiums, exposition buildings, new city halls, new post offices, roads, even monuments.

A passion to build possessed them. Under the head of housing they completed in the one year 1930 more than 300,000 habitations. The great weight of new housing was for wage workers, state servants, and people of moderate means. Any new housing project in the mass principle is called a settlement. So, workers' settlements, railway employees' settlements, post office employees' settlements, bachelors' settlements. But settlements also in selected places for the well-to-do. What we should call real estate developments on a very large scale. The aggregate is prodigious. The only way to see it really is from the air because one settlement or one series of flat dwellings may be the size of a town. Moreover, you would have to drive an endless distance to see it from the ground. It is in character extensive, and in new places. The cities have not been rebuilt. They have not changed much. These people do not tear down old things to build new ones. For new things new ground. All this change is in the environs.

The building passion overflowed necessity, became extravagant, experimental, sportive. New time, new materials, new shapes, new measures, new intentions. Churches all of steel and glass. The modernistic extreme in villas, morgues, hotels, schools, skyscrapers, commercial buildings. It was an architect's festival.

Many creditors are scandalized by the signs of Germany's extravagance with borrowed money, the French and the English more than Americans, since they have less understanding of extravagance in principle. The Germans admit it. They may say truthfully that they have been heard to denounce it themselves, to one another. All the same, they went on with it. And then, too, great sums were purposefully spent for the future, as for a new fourth bridge across the Rhine at Cologne, now one of the engineering marvels of Europe.

The French said: "There is no present necessity for this bridge. Why do you build it? You do not pay reparations with a bridge."

The Germans said: "We shall sometime need it, and we build it now to keep our people employed."

It was their instinct, or their wisdom, to increase their power and improve their conditions by any means possible, even though it was with creditors' money they did it. And from their own point of view they were right. What they have built they will continue to possess. Gold they may lose; credit they may lose. But machines, factories, power plants, bridges, public buildings, roads, laboratories, better dwellings, parks—these things remain. They cannot fly away. What happens to the money seems relatively unimportant. Money is not things. It is merely the token of things. Destroy the token and there are the things still, physically untouched by a financial crisis. You can invent new tokens to represent them. That has happened before. Less than ten years ago was not German money wholly destroyed? The things it had represented, they were not destroyed, not even German credit, which was an intangible thing. A new money token was invented in place of the one that had been destroyed, and lo! Germany was in good credit again, the whole world anxious to become her creditor.

Moreover, by what may seem to have been reckless and extravagant use of borrowed money, Germany has created a great body of social wealth, visible as fine housing, recreational facilities, and other means to human well-being, the existence of which tends to defeat what impulse there may have been to communism. If there was any real danger of communism in Germany, which is doubtful, it is greatly lessened by the fact that the German wage workers have much more comfort, well-being, and freedom of ego to defend than ever before.

The red menace in all political senses is probably seven-tenths conjuration.[1] The communists are four or five million all together. But they have no leadership. There is not one important mind among them. There is an idea in Germany that the rulers of Soviet Russia do not want Germany to go red—at least not yet. They are too fearful of the effect it might have on her efficiency and productive power and too anxious for the present to draw upon that efficiency and power for their own needs. Whether this is true or not, the Russians would be very intelligent to take that view and to maintain in Germany merely a tin façade of communism, numerically strong, politically weak.

The well-poised German's view of communism is first of all cynical. He says: "It is something to have in the hand." He means that when the German government is having difficulties with the Reichstag it can rally supporters by waving the red menace or threatening to take support from the communists; and that when German statesmen are dealing with the outside world, as at the London conference, they can say: "Responsible government has its back to the wall in Germany. Uphold us for your own sake as much as for ours, for if this government falls we shall all of us have to face communism in Germany." And it works. It has been working ever since the armistice.

None but a German can understand the involutions of German politics, and there is reason to doubt that a German does. Parties beginning at the center and shading right and left, parties within parties, parties left of the right and parties right of the left, all in a ceaseless way of quarreling, not about ideas as such but about the philosophy and theory of ideas. Any new idea has first to be examined from the point of view of party advantage, and then, if ever, on its merits. As you look at this ill-natured, monotonous

---

[1]Since this was written Von Hindenburg has been reelected president of the German republic.

eddy of grumbling disagreement, their whole political-mindedness apparently revolving in muddy innocence of realities, you will say it is hopeless, worse than drifting. How can there be a sense of direction among them? But then when you look at what lies behind them in the last ten years and at what they have done with their advantages against the world, you can almost imagine that a Machiavellian intelligence has been guiding them. Look again at the great eddy of political confusion and it may occur to you that here their disagreements cancel one another and all their passion for petty interference is absorbed, so that beyond it in the field of reality their true intelligence, their racial intuition, or whatever it is that leads them is all the more free to act upon their destiny, without interference.

For example, during the July 1931 crisis they passed from a republican form of government to a dictatorship and were hardly aware of it. The constitution was suspended in fact; they were governed by decree, their parliament was in a state of self-abnegation, employers were ordered to withhold fifty percent of wages due, scores of newspapers were shut up, a German could not cross the border without paying first a fine of twenty-five dollars, free comment touching the German chancellor's work at London was *verboten* lest it interfere with the result—and there was no protest. Under the circumstances a dictatorship was necessary. It could set itself up automatically. No party was responsible for it; therefore, no party cared. And the interminable sounds issuing from the eddy were the same as before.

And if Germany did go red, in a political sense, it would not be like Russian communism. The Germans have not the heart to destroy their own things. They overthrew a monarchy and destroyed nothing. It never occurred to them to destroy its human symbol, namely, the kaiser. He was exiled on a pension, partly to appease the world; he was unwept because he had failed. But the crown prince was received back and now is active in German politics, at the extreme right. Least of all would the Germans destroy their tools, that is to say, their own industrial power, for that is their first source of hope.

Yet notwithstanding the reduction of the red menace, it it was real, and notwithstanding the social improvement in Germany, which is very real, many creditors are still scandalized. They keep saying: "From the German point of view, yes; but it was borrowed money. They spent it for such things as even the lenders cannot always afford. They must have known as they were spending it that they would be unable to pay it back when it was due.''

That is not exactly what they know. They probably thought very little about it; and, moreover, if they had thought about it they would not have cared. To understand this it will be necessary to go further with the German point of view.

To begin with, most of the money was coming from American lenders, and every German has it in his heart that his country was beaten by America, not by the Allies. But for the vast weight of American resources, first as they were loaned to the Allies and then as they went directly into the war, German victory had been inevitable, according to destiny. American money thwarted that destiny.

Then consider the emotional conviction under which now every process of the German mind takes place. How it was arrived at does not matter as a practical fact. The conviction is that there was a conspiracy to crush Germany. It did not succeed. Yet there will be no justice in the world until the Treaty of Versailles is destroyed; and the special infamy of that document is that it contains a confession of guilt extorted from a people reduced to their knees by the power of the whole world.

It follows that they have no sense of debt on account of reparations. Simply, reparations are tribute. It follows also that the secret German language about Germany's principal creditors may be extremely ironical, with some special emphasis toward Americans, from whom it was so easy to borrow money to pay tribute with. How could they be expected to care very much about what happened to the money they borrowed? It was the money of their enemies, and as they were borrowing and spending it to increase their power they were counting the years the war had lasted—fourteen, fifteen, sixteen. And what a stupid world of lenders!

The finality of all fact about the Germans is that they have the feelings, the mentality, and the motives of an injured race. Their sense of injury is obsessional, so deep and so ugly as to seem a national psychosis, as it probably is. Germany against the world is the one thought that will unite them; and that never fails. Self-commiseration is their emotional habit.

They believe it themselves when they tell you Germany is poor.

You must not be deceived by appearances. There is bitter distress just beneath the surface. There is no fat, or, if there is, then it is not good fat. Germany's tissues are white, if you could only see them. Reparations do that. She is helpless; she is at the mercy of her creditors. Her middle class has been destroyed. Can you destroy a middle class without suffering? People come to look. They see Germans eating and bathing and trying to be gay, but this is desperation, the behavior of a people living in fear of deluge. Really it is not so. They are not gay. If the shops are busy that is because they are afraid of their own money and spend it in order to hoard things instead. They remember inflation. And if they go out to dine once more in a good way, it is because they do not know what will happen tomorrow.

One who had heard this theme too much and heard it again from a group of tense, earnest Germans at dinner in Berlin last July, tried turning their minds around.

"I imagine myself to be a German," he said. "The year is 1924. I am gazing at the heavens. Do you remember that after the armistice, or, as other people say, after the war, there came a craze for heaven gazing in Germany? That is when you began to build these wonderful planetariums."

"Yes," they said, a little bewildered.

"I imagine I was a German in 1924," he continued, "at a planetarium, as every one else was, and as I sat gazing at the celestial mechanism, suddenly I saw the future of Germany, clearly, like a dream."

"What was it?" they asked. "What did you see?"

"Wait," he said. "First, do you remember what it was like in 1924? The enemy tarried in the Rhineland, holding it for hostage of good behavior. The French were in the Ruhr, squeezing the very heart of Germany. Foreign commissions were seated in Berlin, watching and minding everything. Germany was insolvent. Her money was worthless. A million marks would hardly buy a cold supper."

The Germans groaned.

"Then the vision," he said. "I imagine that as a German I saw what would happen to Germany in the next six years. I saw that in 1930 she would be free of foreign control, the enemy would be out of the Rhineland, the French would be out of the Ruhr. I saw that in 1930 Germany would be the best-equipped nation in Europe, paramount in Europe for industrial power and second in the world only to the United States. I saw that in 1930 she would be the best-housed nation in Europe, if not in the world. I saw that in 1930 her exports would pass Great Britain's for the first time, and this had been her lifelong ambition. I saw that in 1930 she would hold the blue ribbon of the sea against England, with the two newest and fastest ships on the Atlantic, and that she would have once more a great merchant marine, all new and modern, besides building ships for other nations in successful competition with England's shipbuilding industry. I saw that in 1930 she would be first in aviation among European nations, with the largest land plane in the world, the largest seaplane in the world, and the finest airports. I saw that in 1931 she would be strong enough to say 'no' to the French when as a condition for an international loan they proposed that Germany disband her weaponless army of Steel Helmets and stop building battleships. I saw one of the new 10,000-ton battleships and reflected on the folly of Germany's enemies. They thought to limit the strength of her sea weapons with a piece of writing, which says a German warship shall not exceed 10,000 tons. All they did was to stimulate German inventiveness, for under this limitation she had made a sea weapon in 10,000 tons that was probably equal to any 25,000-ton warship in the world. I saw that in 1931 she would be strong enough to dare say officially, 'Reparations are tribute,' which was notice that she was almost strong enough to repudiate them. And I saw that meanwhile, during six years, she had borrowed much more from her enemies than she had paid them as reparations, which meant that she herself had paid no reparations at all. I saw that in 1931 she would be strong enough, without weapons, to threaten the political peace of Europe and strong enough to threaten the economic rhythm of the world by letting loose the full power of her industries and laboratories. There the vision ended. I imagined I had been asleep. It was a dream. What a fabulous dream! And yet all of it has come true.''

"It has come true," said the Germans, with not the slightest rift in their gloom. It was deeper than ever. "Such things as you mention are true," they said. "But you are not a German. You cannot imagine what it is like. The situation of Germany is desperate."

What were they thinking of then? Their lost colonies? The French empire? The new French fortifications? Their isolation?

The guilt phrase in the Versailles Treaty? You will never know. It may be they were thinking how awkward it was for the stream of American money out of which they had been paying reparations to dry up suddenly. Unless it rises again they may have to decide whether actually to pay something by way of tribute or repudiate reparations before they are quite ready to risk it.

The New Deal
and The International
Monetary System

Murray N. Rothbard

The international monetary policies of the New Deal may be divided into two decisive and determining actions, one at the beginning of the new Deal and the other at its end. The first was its decision, in early 1933, to opt for domestic inflation and monetary nationalism, a course which helped steer the entire world onto a similar path during the remainder of the decade. The second was its thrust, during World War II, to reconstitute an international monetary order, this time built on the dollar as the world's "key" and crucial currency. If we wished to use lurid terminology, we might call these a decision for dollar nationalism and dollar imperialism respectively.

The Background of the 1920s

It is impossible to understand the first New Deal decision for dollar nationalism without setting that choice in the monetary world of the 1920s, from which the New Deal had emerged. Similarly, it is impossible to understand the monetary system of the 1920s without reference to the pre–World War monetary order and its breakup during the war; for the world of the 1920s was an attempt to reconstitute an international monetary order, seemingly one quite similar to the status quo ante, but actually one based on very different principles and institutions.

The prewar monetary order was genuinely "international"; that is, world money rested not on paper tickets issued by one or more governments but on a genuine economic commodity—gold—whose supply rested on market supply-and-demand principles. In short, the international gold standard was the monetary equivalent and corollary of international free trade in commodities. It was a method of separating money from the State just as enterprise and foreign trade had been so separated. In short, the gold standard was the monetary counterpart of laissez-faire in other economic areas.

The gold standard in the prewar era was never "pure," no more than was laissez-faire in general. Every major country, except the United States, had central banks which tried their best to inflate and manipulate the currency. But the system was such that this intervention could only operate within narrow limits. If one country inflated its currency, the inflation in that country would cause the banks to lose gold to other nations, and consequently the banks, private and central, would before long be brought to heel. And while England was the world financial center during this period, its predominance was market rather than political, and so it too had to abide by the monetary discipline of the gold standard. As H. Parker Willis described it,

> Prior to the World War the distribution of the metallic money of gold standard countries had been directed and regulated by the central banks of the world in accordance with the generally known and recognized principles of international distribution of the precious metals. Free movement of these metals and freedom on the part of the individual to acquire and hold them were general. Regulation of foreign exchange... existed only sporad ically,... and was so conducted as not to interfere in any important degree with the disposal of holding of specie by individuals or by banks.[1]

The advent of the World War disrupted and rended this economic idyll, and it was never to return. In the first place, all of the major countries financed the massive war effort through an equally massive inflation, which meant that every country except the United States, even including Great Britain, was forced to go off the gold standard, since they could no longer hope to redeem their currency obligations in gold. The international order was not only sundered by the war, but also split into numerous separate, competing, and warring currencies, whose inflation was no longer subject to the gold restraint. In addition, the various governments engaged in rigorous exchange control, fixing exchange rates and

---

[1]Henry Parker Willis, *The Theory and Practice of Central Banking* (New York: Harper & Bros., 1936), p. 379.

prohibiting outflows of gold; monetary warfare paralleled the broader economic and military conflict.

At the end of the war, the major powers sought to reconstitute some form of international monetary order out of the chaos and warring economic blocs of the war period. The crucial actor in this drama was Great Britain, which was faced with a series of dilemmas and difficulties. On the one hand, Britain not only aimed at reestablishing its former eminence, but it meant to use its victorious position and its domination of the League of Nations to work its will upon the other nations, many of them new and small, of post-Versailles Europe. This meant its monetary as well as its general political and economic dominance. Furthermore, it no longer felt itself bound by old-fashioned laissez-faire restraints from exerting frankly political control, nor did it any longer feel bound to observe the classical gold-standard restraints against inflation.

While Britain's appetite was large, its major dilemma was its weakness of resources. The wracking inflation and the withdrawal from the gold standard had left the United States, not Great Britain, as the only "hard," gold standard country. If Great Britain were to dominate the postwar monetary picture, it would somehow have to take the United States into camp as its willing junior partner. From the classic prewar pound-dollar par of $4.86 to the pound, the pound had fallen on the international money markets to $3.50, a substantial 30 percent drop, a drop which reflected the greater degree of inflation in Great Britain than in the United States. The British then decided to constitute a new form of international monetary system, the "gold exchange standard," which it finally completed in 1925. In the classical, prewar gold standard, each country kept its reserves in gold and redeemed its paper and bank currencies in gold coin upon demand. The new gold exchange standard was a clever device to permit Britain and the other European countries to remain inflated and to continue inflating, while enlisting the United States as the ultimate support for all currencies. Specifically, Great Britain would keep its reserves, not in gold but in dollars, while the smaller countries of Europe would keep *their* reserves, not in gold but in pounds sterling. In this way, Great Britain could pyramid inflated currency and credit on top of dollars, while Britain's client states could pyramid *their* currencies, in turn, on top of pounds. Clearly, this also meant that *only* the United States would remain on a gold coin standard, the other countries "redeeming" only in foreign exchange. The instability of this system, with psuedo–gold standard countries pyramiding on top of an increasingly shaky dollar-gold base, was to become evident in the Great Depression.

But the British task was not simply to induce the United States to be the willing guarantor of all the shaky and inflated currencies of war-torn Europe. For Great Britain might well have been able to return to the original form of gold standard at a new, realistic, depreciated parity of $3.50 to the pound. But it was not willing to do so. For the British dream was to restore, even more glowingly than before, British financial preeminence, and if it depreciated the pound by 30 percent it would thereby acknowledge that the dollar, not the pound, was the world financial center. This it was fiercely unwilling to do; for restoration of dominance, for the saving of financial face; it would return at the good old $4.86 or bust in the attempt. And bust it almost did. For to insist on returning to gold at $4.86, even on the new, vitiated, gold exchange basis, was to mean that the pound would be absurdly expensive in relation to the dollar and other currencies, and would therefore mean that at current inflated price levels, British exports—its economic lifeline—would be severely crippled, and a general depression would ensue. And indeed, Britain suffered a severe depression in her export industries—particularly coal and textiles—throughout the 1920s. If she insisted on returning at the overvalued $4.86, there was only one hope for keeping her exports competitive in price: a massive domestic deflation to lower price and wage levels. While a severe deflation is difficult at best, Britain now found it impossible, for the new system of national unemployment insurance and the newfound strength of trade unions made wage cutting politically unthinkable.

But if Britain would or could not make her exports competitive by returning to gold at a depreciated par or by deflating at home, there was a third alternative which it could pursue, and which indeed marked the key to the British international economic policy of the 1920s: it could induce or force *other* countries to inflate, or themselves to return to gold at overvalued pars; in short, if it could not clean up its own economic mess, it could contrive to impose messes upon everyone else. If it did not do so, it would see inflating Britain lose gold to the United States, France, and other "hard money" countries, as indeed happened during the 1920s; only by contriving for other countries, especially the United States, to inflate also, could it check the loss of gold and therefore halt the collapse of the whole jerry-built international monetary structure.

In the short run, the British scheme was brilliantly conceived, and it worked for a time; but the major problem went unheeded: If the United States, the base of the pyramid and the sole link of all these countries to gold and hard money, were to inflate unduly, the *dollar too* would become shaky, it would lose gold at home and abroad, and the dollar would itself eventually collapse, dragging the entire structure down with it. And this is essentially what happened in the Great Depression.

In Europe, England was able to use its domination of the powerful Financial Committee of the League of Nations to cajole or bludgeon country after country to (a) establish central banks which would collaborate closely with the Bank of England, (b) return to gold *not* in the classical gold coin standard but in the new gold exchange standard which would permit continued inflation by all the countries; and (c) return to this new standard at overvalued pars so that European exports would be hobbled vis-à-vis the exports of Great Britain. The Financial Committee of the league was largely dominated and run by Britain's major financial figure, Montagu Norman, head of the Bank of England, working through such close Norman associates on the committee as Sir Otto Niemeyer and Sir Henry Strakosch, leaders in the concept of close central bank collaboration to "stabilize" (in practice, to raise) price levels throughout the world. The distinguished British economist Sir Ralph Hawtrey, director of financial studies at the British treasury, was one of the first to advocate this system, as well as to call for the general European adoption of a gold exchange standard. In the spring of 1922, Norman induced the league to call the Genoa Conference, which urged similar measures.[2]

But the British scarcely confined their pressure upon European countries to resolutions and conferences. Using the carrot of

---

[2]See Murray N. Rothbard, *America's Great Depression* (3rd Ed. Mission, Kan.: Sheed and Ward, 1975), pp. 159 ff.

loans from England and the United States and the stick of political pressure, Britain induced country after country to order its monetary affairs to suit the British—i.e., to return only to a gold exchange standard at overvalued pars that would hamper their own exports and stimulate imports from Great Britain. Furthermore, the British also used their inflated, cheap credit to lend widely to Europe in order to stimulate their own flagging export market. A trenchant critique of British policy was recorded in the diary of Émile Moreau, governor of the Bank of France, a country which clung to the gold standard and to a hard-money policy, and was thereby instrumental in bringing down the pound and British financial domination in 1931. Moreau wrote:

> ... England having been the first European country to reestablish a stable and secure money [*sic*] has used that advantage to establish a basis for putting Europe under a veritable financial domination. The Financial Committee [of the League of Nations] at Geneva has been the instrument of that policy. The method consists of forcing every country in monetary difficulty to subject itself to the Committee at Geneva, which the British control. The remedies prescribed always involve the installation in the central bank of a foreign supervisor who is British or designated by the Bank of England, and the deposit of a part of the reserve of the central bank at the Bank of England, which serves both to support the pound and to fortify British influence. To guarantee against possible failure they are careful to secure the cooperation of the Federal Reserve Bank of New York. Moreover, they pass on to America the task of making some of the foreign loans if they seem too heavy, always retaining the political advantage of these operations.
>
> England is thus completely or partially entrenched in Austria, Hungary, Belgium, Norway, and Italy. She is in the process of entrenching herself in Greece and Portugal. She seeks to get a foothold in Yugoslavia and fights us cunningly in Rumania.... The currencies will be divided into two classes. Those of the first class, the dollar and the pound sterling, based on gold and those of the second class based on the pound and the dollar—with a part of their gold reserves being held by the Bank of England and the Federal Reserve Bank of New York. The latter moneys will have lost their independence.[3]

---

[3]Émile Moreau diary, entry of February 6, 1928. Lester V. Chandler, *Benjamin Strong: Central Banker* (Washington, D.C.: The Brookings Institution, 1958) pp. 379–80. On the gold exchange standard, and European countries being induced to overvalue their currencies, see H. Parker Willis, "The Breakdown of the Gold Exchange Standard and its Financial Imperialism," *The Annalist* (October 16, 1931),

Inducing the United States to support and bolster the pound and the gold exchange system was vital to Britain's success, and this cooperation was insured by the close ties that developed between Montagu Norman and Benjamin Strong, governor of the Federal Reserve Bank of New York, who had seized effective and nearly absolute control of Federal Reserve operations from his appointment at the inception of the Fed in 1914 until his death in 1928. This control over the Fed was achieved over the opposition of the Federal Reserve Board in Washington, who generally opposed or grumbled at Strong's Anglophile policies. Strong and Norman made annual trips to visit each other, all of which were kept secret not only from the public but from the Federal Reserve Board itself.

Strong and the Federal Reserve Bank of New York propped up England and the gold exchange standard in numerous ways. One was direct lines of credit, which the New York Bank extended, in 1925 and after, to Britain, Belgium, Poland, and Italy, to subsidize their going to a gold exchange standard at overvalued pars. More directly significant was a massive monetary inflation and credit expansion which Strong generated in the United States in 1924 and again in 1927, for the purpose of propping up the pound. The idea was that gold flows from Britain to the United States would be checked and reversed by American credit expansion, which would prop up or raise prices of American goods, thereby stimulating imports from Great Britain, and also lower interest rates in the United States as compared to Britain. The fall in interest rates would further stimulate flows of gold from the United States to Britain and thereby check the results of British inflation and overvaluation of the pound. Both times, the inflationary injection worked and prevented Britain from reaping the results of its own inflationary policies, but at the high price of inflation in the United States, a dangerous stock market and real estate boom, and an eventual depression. At the secret central-bank conference of July 1927 in New York, called at the behest of Norman, Strong agreed to this inflationary credit expansion over the objections of

---

pp. 626 ff.; and William Adams Brown, Jr., *The International Gold Standard Reinterpreted,* 1914–1934 (New York: National Bureau of Economic Research, 1940), II, pp. 732–749.

Germany and France, and Strong gaily told the French representative that he was going to give "a little *coup de whiskey* to the stock market." It was a coup for which America and the world would pay dearly.[4]

The Chicago business and financial community, not having Strong's ties with England, protested vigorously against the 1927 expansion, and the Federal Reserve Bank of Chicago held out as long as it could against the expansion of cheap money and the lowering of interest rates. The Chicago *Tribune* went so far as to call for Strong's resignation and perceptively charged that discount rates were being lowered in the interests of Great Britain. Strong, however, sold the policy to the Middle West with the rationale that its purpose was to help the American farmer by means of cheap credit. In contrast, the English financial community hailed the work of Norman in securing Strong's support, and *The Banker* of London lauded Strong as "one of the best friends England ever had." *The Banker* praised the "energy and skillfullness he [Strong] has given to the service of England" and exulted that "his name should be associated with that of Mr. [Walter Hines] Page as a friend of England in her greatest need."[5]

A blatant example of Strong's intervention to help Norman and his policy occurred in the spring of 1926, when one of Norman's influential colleagues proposed a full gold-coin standard in India. At Norman's request, Strong and a team of American economists rushed to England to ward off the plan, testifying that a gold drain to India would check inflation in other countries, and instead successfully backed the Norman policy of a gold exchange

[4]On the *coup de whiskey*, see Charles Rist, "Notice Biographique," *Revue d'Economie Politique* (November-December 1955), p. 1005. (Translation mine.) On the Strong-Norman collaboration, also see Lawrence E. Clark, *Central Banking Under the Federal Reserve System* (New York: Macmillan, 1935), pp. 307-321; and Benjamin M. Anderson, *Economics and the Public Welfare: Financial and Economic History of the United States,* 1914-1946 (New York: D. Van Nostrand, 1949).

[5]*The Banker,* June 1, 1926, and November 1928. In Clark, *Central Banking,* pp. 315-16. Also see Anderson, *Economics and the Public Welfare,* pp. 182-83; Benjamin H. Beckhart, "Federal Reserve Policy and the Money Market, 1923-1931," in Beckhart et al., *The New York Money Market* (New York: Columbia University Press, 1931), IV, pp. 67 ff. In the autumn of 1926, a leading American banker admitted that bad consequences would follow Strong's cheap money policy, but added: "that cannot be helped. It is the price we must pay for helping Europe." H. Parker Willis, "The Failure of the Federal Reserve," *North American Review* (1929), p. 553.

standard and domestic "economizing" of gold to permit domestic expansion of credit.[6]

The intimate Norman-Strong collaboration for joint inflation and the gold exchange standard was not at all an accident of personality; it was firmly grounded on the close ties that both of them had with the House of Morgan and the Morgan interests. Strong himself was a product of the Morgan nexus; he had been the head of the Morgan-oriented Bankers' Trust Company before becoming governor of the New York Fed, and his closest ties were with Morgan partners Henry P. Davison and Dwight Morrow, who induced him to assume his post at the Federal Reserve. J. P. Morgan and Co., in turn, was an agent of the British government and of the Bank of England, and its close financial ties with England, its loans to England, and tie-ins with the American export trade had been highly influential in inducing the United States to enter the World War on England's side.[7] As for Montagu Norman, his grandfather had been a partner in the London banking firm of Brown, Shipley, & Co., and of the affiliated New York firm of Brown Brothers & Co., a powerful investment banking firm long associated with the House of Morgan. Norman himself had been a partner of Brown, Shipley and had worked for several years in the offices of Brown Brothers in the United States.

Moreover, J. P. Morgan and Co. played a direct collaborative role with the New York Fed, lending $100 million of its own to Great Britain to facilitate its return to gold, and also collaborating in futile loans to prop up the shaky European banking system during the financial crisis of 1931. It is no wonder that in his study of the Federal Reserve System during the pre–New Deal era, Dr. Clark concluded "that the New York Reserve Bank in collaboration with a private international banking house [J. P. Morgan and Co.], determined the policy to be followed by the Federal Reserve System."[8]

The major theoretical rationale employed by Strong and Norman was the idea of governmental collaboration to "stabilize"

[6]See Rothbard, *America's Great Depression,* p. 138; and Chandler, *Benjamin Strong,* pp. 356 ff.

[7]Charles Callan Tansill, *America Goes To War* (Boston: Little, Brown and Co., 1938), pp. 70–134. On the aid given by Benjamin Strong to the House of Morgan and the loans to England and France, see ibid., pp. 87–88, 96–101, 106–8, 118–32.

[8]Clark, *Central Banking,* p. 343.

the price level. The laissez-faire policy of the classical, prewar gold standard meant that prices would be allowed to find their own level in accordance with supply and demand, and without interference by central bank manipulation. In practice, this meant a secularly falling price level, as the supply of goods rose over time in accordance with the long-run rise in productivity. And *in practice,* price stabilization really meant price *raising*: either keeping prices up when they were falling, or "reflating" prices by raising them through inflationary action by the central banks. Price stabilization therefore meant the replacement of the classical, laissez-faire gold standard by "managed money," by inflationary credit expansion stimulated by the central banks.

In England, it was, as we have seen, no accident that the lead in advocating price stabilization was taken by Sir Ralph Hawtrey and various associates of Montagu Norman, including Sir Josiah Stamp, chairman of Midland Railways and a director of the Bank of England, and two other prominent directors—Sir Basil Blackett and Sir Charles Addis.

It has long been a myth of American historiography that bankers and big businessmen are invariably believers in "hard money" as against cheap credit or inflation. This was certainly not the experience of the New Deal or the pre–New Deal era.[9] While the most articulate leaders of the price stabilizationists were academic economists led by Professor Irving Fisher of Yale, Fisher was able to enlist in his Stable Money League (founded 1921) and its successor Stable Money Association, a host of men of wealth, bankers and businessmen, as well as labor and farm leaders. Among those serving as officers of the league and association were: Henry Agard Wallace, editor of *Wallace's Farmer* and secretary of agriculture in the New Deal; the wealthy John G. Winant, later governor of New Hampshire; George Eastman of the Eastman-Kodak family; Frederick H. Goff, head of the Cleveland Trust Company; John E. Rovensky, executive vice-president of the Bank of America; Frederic Delano, uncle of

---

[9]For examples of businessmen and bankers in favor of cheap money and inflation in American history, and particularly on the inflationary role of Paul M. Warburg of Kuhn, Loeb and Co. during the 1920s, see Murray N. Rothbard, "Money, the State, and Modern Mercantilism," in H. Schoeck and J. W. Wiggins, eds., *Central Planning and Neo-Mercantilism* (Princeton, N.J.: D. Van Nostrand, 1964), pp. 146–54.

Franklin D. Roosevelt; Samuel Gompers, John P. Frey, and William Green of the American Federation of Labor; Paul M. Warburg, partner of Kuhn, Loeb and Co.; Otto H. Kahn, prominent investment banker; James H. Rand, Jr., head of Remington Rand Company, and Owen D. Young of General Electric. Furthermore, the heads of the following organizations agreed to serve as ex-officio honorary vice-presidents of the Stable Money Association: the American Association for Labor Legislation; the American Bar Association; the American Farm Bureau Federation; the Brotherhood of Railroad Trainmen; the National Association of Credit Men; the National Association of Owners of Railroad and Public Utility Securities; the National Retail Dry Goods Association; the United States Building and Loan League; the American Cotton Growers Exchange; the Chicago Association of Commerce; the Merchants Association of New York; and the heads of the Bankers' Association of forty-three states and the District of Columbia.[10]

Irving Fisher was unsurprisingly exultant over the supposed achievement of Governor Strong in stabilizing the wholesale price level during the late 1920s, and he led American economists in trumpeting the "New Era" of permanent prosperity which the new policy of managed money was assuring to America and the world. Fisher was particularly critical of the minority of skeptical economists who warned of overexpansion in the stock and real estate markets due to cheap money, and even after the stock market crash Fisher continued to insist that prosperity, particularly in the stock market, was just around the corner. Fisher's partiality toward stock market inflation was perhaps not unrelated to his own personal role as a millionaire investor in the stock market, a role in which he was financially dependent on a cheap money policy.[11] In the general enthusiasm for Strong and the New Era of monetary and stock market inflation, the minority of skeptics was led by the Chase National Bank, affiliated with the Rockefeller interests, particularly A. Barton Hepburn, economic historian and chairman of the board of the bank, and its chief economist Dr.

[10]Irving Fisher, *Stabilised Money* (London: George Allen & Unwin, 1935), pp. 104–13, 375–89, 411–12.

[11]Fisher was also a partner of James H. Rand, Jr., in a card-index manufacturing firm. Ibid., pp. 387–88; Irving Norton Fisher, *My Father Irving Fisher* (New York: Comet Press, 1956), pp. 220 ff.

Benjamin M. Anderson, Jr. Another highly influential and indefatigable critic was Dr. H. Parker Willis, editor of the *Journal of Commerce,* formerly aide to Senator Carter Glass (D., Va.), and professor of banking at Columbia University, along with Willis's numerous students, who included Dr. Ralph W. Robey, later to become economist at the National Association of Manufacturers. Another critic was Dr. Rufus S. Tucker, economist at General Motors. On the Federal Reserve Board the major critic was Dr. Adolph C. Miller, a close friend of Herbert Hoover, who joined in the criticisms of the Strong policy. On the other hand, Secretary of Treasury Andrew W. Mellon, of the powerful Mellon interests, enthusiastically backed the inflationist policy. This split in the nation's leading banking and business circles was to foreshadow the split over Franklin Roosevelt's monetary departures in 1933.

The First New Deal: Dollar Nationalism

The international monetary framework of the 1920s collapsed in the storm of the Great Depression; or rather, it collapsed of its own inner contradictions in a depression which it had helped to bring about. For one of the most calamitous features of the depression was the international wave of banking failures; and the banks failed from the inflation and overexpansion which were the fruits of the managed international gold exchange standard. Once the jerry-built pyramiding of bank credit had collapsed, it brought down the banking system of nation after nation; as inflation led to a piling up of currency claims abroad, the cashing in of claims led to a well-founded suspicion of the solvency of other banks, and so the failures spread and intensified. The failures in the weak currency countries led to the accumulation of strains in other weak currency nations, and, ultimately, on the bases of the shaky pyramid: Britain and the United States.

The major banking crisis began with the near bankruptcy in 1929 of the Boden-Kredit-Anstalt of Vienna, the major bank in Austria, which had never recovered from its dismemberment at Versailles. Desperate attempts by J. P. Morgan, the House of Rothschild, and later the New York Fed, to shore up the bank only succeeded in a temporary rescue which committed more financial resources to an unsound bank and thereby made its ultimate failure in May 1931 all the more catastrophic. Rather than permit the outright liquidation of its banking systems, Austria, followed by Germany and other European countries, went off the gold standard during 1931.[12]

But the key to the international monetary situation was Great Britain, the nub and the base for the world's gold exchange standard. British inflation and cheap money, and the standard which had made Britain the base of the world's money, put enormous pressure on the pound sterling, as foreign holders of sterling balances became increasingly panicky and called on the British to redeem their sterling in either gold or dollars. The heavy loans by British banks to Germany during the 1920s made the pressure after the German monetary collapse still more severe. But Britain *could* have saved the day by using the classical gold standard medicine in such crises: by raising bank interest rates sharply, thereby attracting funds to Britain from other countries. In such monetary crises, furthermore, such temporary tight money and check to inflation gives foreigners confidence that the pound will be sustained, and they then continue to hold sterling without calling on the country for redemption. In earlier crises, for example, Britain had raised its bank rate as high as 10 percent early in the proceedings, and temporarily contracted the money supply to put a stringent check to inflation. But by 1931 deflation and hard money had become unthinkable in the British political climate. And so Britain stunned the financial world by keeping its bank rate very low, never raising it above 4½ percent, and in fact continuing to inflate sterling still further to offset gold losses abroad. As the run on sterling inevitably intensified, Great Britain cynically repudiated its own gold exchange standard, the very monetary standard that it had forced and cajoled Europe to adopt, by coolly going off the gold standard in September 1931. Its own international monetary system was sacrificed on the altar of continued domestic inflation.[13]

The European monetary system was thereby broken up into

[12]See Anderson, *Economics and the Public Welfare,* pp. 232 ff.

[13]See Lionel Robbins, *The Great Depression* (New York: Macmillan, 1934), pp. 88–99. See also Anderson, *Economics and the Public Welfare,* pp. 244 ff.; and Frederic Benham, *British Monetary Policy* (London: P. S. King & Son, 1932), pp. 1–45.

separate and even warring currency blocs, replete with fluctuating exchange rates, exchange control, and trade restrictions. The major countries followed Britain off the gold standard, with the exception of Belgium, Holland, France, Italy, Switzerland, and the United States. Currency blocs formed with the British Empire forming a sterling bloc, with parities mutually fixed in relation to the pound. It is particularly ironic that one of the earliest effects of Britain's going off gold was that the overvalued pound, now free to fluctuate, fell to its genuine economic value, at or below $3.40 to the pound. And so Britain's grand experiment in returning to a form of gold at an overvalued par had ended in disaster, for herself as well as for the rest of the world.

In the last weeks of the Hoover administration, a desperate attempt was made by the United States to restore an international monetary system; this time the offer was made to Britain to return to the gold standard at the current, eminently more sensible par, in exchange for substantial reduction of the British war debt. No longer would Britain be forced by overvaluation to be in a chronic state of depression of its export industries. But Britain now had the nationalist bit in its teeth, and it insisted on outright "reflation" of prices back up to the predepression, 1929 levels. It had become increasingly clear that the powerful "price stabilizationists" were interested not so much in stabilization as in high prices, and now they would only be satisfied with an inflationary return to boom prices. Britain's rejection of the American offer proved to be fatal for any hopes of international monetary stability.[14]

The world's monetary fate finally rested with the United States, the major gold standard country still remaining. Federal Reserve attempts to inflate the money supply and to lower interest rates during the depression further weakened confidence in the dollar, and gold outflows combined with runs and failures of the banks to put increasing pressure on the American banking system. Finally, during the interregnum between the Hoover and Roosevelt administrations, the nation's banks began to collapse in earnest. The general bank collapse meant that the banking system, always unsound and incapable of paying more than a fraction of its liabilities on demand, could only go in either of two opposite

---

[14]Robbins, *The Great Depression,* pp. 100–121.

directions. A truly laissez-faire policy would have allowed the failing banks to collapse, and thereby to engage in a swift, sharp surgical operation that would have transformed the nation's monetary system from an unsound, inflationary one to a truly "hard" and stable currency. The other pole was for the government to declare massive "bank holidays," i.e., to relieve the banks of the obligation to pay their debts, and then move on to the repudiation of the gold standard and its replacement by inflated fiat paper issued by the government. It is important to realize that neither the Hoover nor the Roosevelt administrations had any intention of taking the first route. While there was a considerable split on whether or not to stay on the gold standard, no one endorsed the rigorous laissez-faire route.[15]

The new Roosevelt administration was now faced with the choice of retaining or going off the gold standard. While almost everyone supported the temporary "bank holidays," there was a severe split on the longer run question of the monetary standard.

While the bulk of the nation's academic economists stood staunchly behind the gold standard, the indefatigable Irving Fisher redoubled his agitation for inflation, spurred onward by his personal desire to reinflate stock prices. Since the Stable Money Association had been supposedly dedicated to price stabilization, and what Fisher and the inflationists wanted was a drastic raising of prices, the association liquidated its assets into the new and frankly inflationist "Committee for the Nation to Rebuild Prices and Purchasing Power." The Committee for the Nation, founded in January 1933, stood squarely for the "reflation" of prices back to their pre-1929 levels; stabilization of the price level was to proceed only *after* that point had been achieved. The Committee for the Nation, which was to prove crucially influential on Roosevelt's decision, was composed largely of prominent businessmen. The committee was originated by Vincent Bendix, president of Bendix Aviation, and General Robert E. Wood, head of Sears, Roebuck and Co. They were soon joined, in the fall of 1932, by Frank A. Vanderlip, long close to Fisher and formerly president of the National City Bank of New York, by James H. Rand, Jr., of Remington Rand, and by Magnus W.

---

[15]See Rothbard, *America's Great Depression,* pp. 284–99; H. Parker Willis, "A Crisis in American Banking," in H. P. Willis and J. M. Chapman, eds., *The Banking Situation* (New York: Columbia University Press, 1934), pp. 3–120.

Alexander, head of the National Industrial Conference Board.

Other members of the Committee for the Nation included: Fred H. Sexauer, president of the Dairymen's League Cooperative Association; Frederic H. Frazier, chairman of the board of the General Baking Company; automobile magnate E. L. Cord; Lessing J. Rosenwald, chairman, Sears, Roebuck; Samuel S. Fels, of Fels and Co.; Philip K. Wrigley, president of William Wrigley Co.; John Henry Hammond, chairman of the board of Bangor & Aroostook R. R.; Edward A. O'Neal, head of the American Farm Bureau Federation, and L. J. Taber, head of the National Grange; F. R. Wurlitzer, vice-president of Rudolph Wurlitzer Mfg. Co.; William J. McAveeny, president of Hudson Motor Co.; Frank E. Gannett of the Gannett Newspapers; and Indiana banker William A. Wirt. Interestingly enough, this same group of highly conservative industrialists was later to become the Committee for Constitutional Government, the major anti–New Deal propaganda group of the late 1930s and 1940s. Yet the Committee was the major proponent of the inflationist policy of the early New Deal in reflating and abandoning the gold standard.

Also associated with the Committee for the Nation was another leading influence on Franklin Roosevelt's decision: agricultural economist George F. Warren of Cornell, who, along with his colleague Frank A. Pearson, was the inspiration for the reflationist Roosevelt program of continually raising the buying price of gold.

The Committee for the Nation at first included several hundred industrial and agricultural leaders, and within a year its membership reached over two thousand. Its recommendations, beginning with going off gold and embargoing gold exports, and continuing through devaluing the dollar and raising the price of gold, were fairly closely followed by the Roosevelt administration.[16] For his part, Irving Fisher, in response to a request for advice by President-elect Roosevelt, had strongly urged at the end of February a frankly inflationist policy of reflation, devaluation, and leaving the gold standard without delay.[17] By April 19, when Roosevelt had cast the die for this policy, Fisher exulted that "Now I *am* sure—as far as we ever can be sure of anything—that

---

[16]Irving Fisher, *Stabilised Money*, pp. 108-9, 118-22, 413-14; Jordan Schwarz, ed., *1933: Roosevelt's Decision: The United States Leaves The Gold Standard* (New York: Chelsea House, 1969), pp. 44-60, 116-20.

[17]Schwarz, *1933: Roosevelt's Decision*, pp. 27-35.

we are going to snap out of this depression fast. I am now one of the happiest men in the world..." In the same letter to his wife, an heiress of the substantial Hazard family fortune, Fisher added: "My next big job is to raise money for ourselves. Probably we'll have to go to Sister again [his wife's sister Caroline]...I have defaulted payments the last few weeks, because I did not think it was fair to ask Sister for money when there was a real chance that I could never pay it back. I mean that if F.D.R. had followed Glass we would have been pretty surely ruined. So would Allied Chemical [in which much of his wife's family fortune was invested], and the U.S. Govt....*Now* I can go to Sister with a clean conscience...."[18]

If Irving Fisher's interest was personal as well as ideological, economic interests also underlay the concern of the Committee for the Nation. The farm groups wanted farm prices driven up, including farm export prices, which necessarily increase in terms of other currencies whenever a currency is devalued. As for the rest of the committee and other inflationists, Herbert Feis notes:

> By the spring of 1933 diverse organizations and groups were crying aloud for some kind of monetary inflation or devaluation, or both. Most effective, probably, was the Committee for the Nation. Among its members were prominent merchants, such as the head of Sears, Roebuck, some journalists, some Wall Street operators and some foreign exchange speculators. Their purpose was to get the United States off the gold standard and to bring about devaluation of the dollar from which they would profit either as speculators in foreign exchange or as businessmen. Another group, more conservative, who stood to gain by devaluation were those who had already exported gold or otherwise acquired liquid deposits in foreign banks. They conceived that they were merely protecting the value of their capital....Then there were the exporters—especially of farm products—who had been at a disadvantage ever since Great Britain had gone off the gold standard and the value of sterling had fallen much below its previous parity with the dollar.[19]

Also advocating and endorsing the decision to inflate and leave the gold standard were such conservative bankers as James P. Warburg of Kuhn, Loeb & Co., one of Roosevelt's leading monetary advisors; former Vice-President and Chicago banker

[18] Irving Norton Fisher, *My Father Irving Fisher,* pp. 273–76.
[19] Herbert Feis, *1933: Characters in Crisis,* in Schwarz, *1933: Roosevelt's Decision,* pp. 150–51. Feis was a leading economist for the State Department.

Charles G. Dawes; Melvin A. Traylor, president of the First National Bank of Chicago; Frank Altschul of the international banking house of Lazard Frères; and Russell C. Leffingwell, partner of J. P. Morgan & Co. Leffingwell told Roosevelt that his action "was vitally necessary and the most important of all the helpful things you have done."[20] Morgan himself hailed Roosevelt's decision to leave the gold standard:

> I welcome the reported action of the President and the Secretary of the Treasury in placing an embargo on gold exports. It has become evident that the effort to maintain the exchange value of the dollar at a premium as against depreciated foreign currencies was having a deflationary effect upon already severely deflated American prices and wages and employment. It seems to me clear that the way out of the depression is to combat and overcome the deflationary forces. Therefore I regard the action now taken as being the best possible course under the circumstances.[21]

Other prominent advocates of going off gold were publishers J. David Stern and William Randolph Hearst, financier James H. R. Cromwell, and Dean Wallace Donham of the Harvard Business School. Conservative Republican senators such as David A. Reed (Pa.) and minority leader Charles L. McNary (Ore.) also approved the decision, and Senator Arthur Vandenberg (R., Mich.) happily declared that Americans could now compete in the export trade "for the first time in many, many months." Vandenberg concluded that "abandonment of the dollar externally may prove to be a complete answer to our problem, so far as the currency factor is concerned."[22]

Amidst this chorus of approval from leading financiers and industrialists, there was still determined opposition to going off gold. Aside from the bulk of the nation's economists, the lead in opposition was again taken by two economists with close ties to the banking community who had been major opponents of the Strong-Morgan policies during the 1920s: Dr. Benjamin M. Anderson of the Rockefeller-oriented Chase National Bank, and Dr. H. Parker Willis, editor of the *Journal of Commerce* and

[20]Arthur M. Schlesinger, Jr., *The Coming of the New Deal* (Boston: Houghton Mifflin, 1959), p. 202.

[21]*New York Times,* April 19, 1933. Quoted in Joseph E. Reeve, *Monetary Reform Movements* (Washington, D.C.: American Council on Public Affairs, 1943), p. 275.

[22]Schwarz, *1933: Roosevelt's Decision,* p. xx.

chief adviser to Senator Carter Glass (D., Va.), who had been secretary of the treasury under Wilson. The Chamber of Commerce of the United States also vigorously attacked the abandonment of gold as well as price level stabilization, and the Chamber of Commerce of New York State also called for prompt return to gold.[23] From the financial community, leading opponents of Roosevelt's decision were Winthrop W. Aldrich, a Rockefeller kinsman, and head of the Chase National Bank, and Roosevelt's budget director Lewis W. Douglas, of the Arizona mining family, who was related to the J. Henry Schroder international bankers and was eventually to become head of Mutual Life Insurance Co. and ambassador to England. Douglas fought valiantly but in vain within the administration against going off gold and against the remainder of the New Deal program.[24]

By the end of April 1933, the United States was clearly off the gold standard, and the dollar quickly began to depreciate relative to gold and the gold standard currencies. Britain, which a few weeks earlier had loftily rejected the idea of international stabilization, now became frightened: currency blocs and a depreciating pound to aid British exports was one thing; depreciation of the dollar to spur American exports and injure British exports was quite another. The British had the presumption to scold the United States for going off gold; they now rested their final hope for a restored international monetary system on the World Economic Conference scheduled for London in June 1933.[25]

Preparations for the conference had been underway for a year, under the guidance of the League of Nations, in a desperate attempt to aid the world economic and financial crisis by attempting the "restoring [of] the currencies on a healthy basis."[26] The Hoover administration was planning to urge the restoration of the international gold standard, but the abandonment of gold by the

---

[23]Irving Fisher, *Stabilised Money*, pp. 355-56.

[24]On Douglas, see Schwarz, *1933: Roosevelt's Decision*, pp. 135-36, 143-44, 154-58; and Schlesinger, *Coming of the New Deal*, pp. 196-97 and *passim*. Douglas resigned as Budget Director in 1934; his critical assessment of the New Deal can be found in his *The Liberal Tradition* (New York: D. Van Nostrand, 1935).

[25]Robbins, *The Great Depression*, p. 123; Schwarz, *1933: Roosevelt's Decision*, p. 144.

[26]Leo Pasvolsky, *Current Monetary Issues* (Washington, D.C.: The Brookings Institution, 1933), p. 14.

Roosevelt administration in March and April, 1933, changed the American position radically. As the conference loomed ahead, it was clear that there were three fundamental positions: the gold bloc—the countries still on the gold standard, headed by France—which desired immediate return to a full international gold standard with fixed exchange rates between the major currencies and gold; the United States, which now placed greatest stress on domestic inflation of the price level; and the British, supported by their Dominions, who wished some form of combination of the two. What was still unclear was whether a satisfactory compromise between these divergent views could be worked out.

At the invitation of President Roosevelt, Prime Minister Ramsay MacDonald of Great Britain and leading statesmen of the other major countries journeyed to Washington for individual talks with the president. All that emerged from these conversations were vague agreements of intent; but the most interesting aspect of the talks was an American proposal, originated by William C. Bullitt and rejected by the French, to establish a coordinated worldwide inflation and devaluation of currencies.

> ...there was serious discussion of a proposal, sponsored by the United States and vigorously opposed by the gold countries, that the whole world should embark upon a "cheaper money" policy, not only through a vigorous and concerted program of credit expansion and the stimulation of business enterprise by means of public works, but also through a simultaneous devaluation, by a fixed percentage, of all currencies which were still at their pre-depression parities.[27]

The American delegation to London was a mixed bag, but the conservative gold standard forces could take heart from the fact that staff economic advisor was James P. Warburg, who had been working eagerly on a plan for international currency stabilization based on gold at new and realistic parities. Furthermore, conservative Professor Oliver M. W. Sprague and George L. Harrison, governor of the New York Fed, were sent to discuss proposals for temporary stabilization of the major currencies. In contrast, the president paid no attention to the petition of eighty-five congressmen, including ten senators, that he appoint as his economic advisor to the conference the radical inflationist and

---

[27]Ibid., p. 59.

antigold priest, Father Charles E. Coughlin.[28]

The World Economic Conference, attended by delegates from sixty-four major nations, opened in London on June 12. The first crisis occurred over the French suggestion for a temporary "currency truce"—a de facto stabilization of exchange rates between the franc, dollar, and pound for the duration of the conference. Surely eminently reasonable, the plan was also a clever device for an entering wedge toward a hopefully permanent stabilization of exchange rates on a full gold basis. The British were amenable, provided that the pound remained fairly cheap in relation to the dollar, so that their export advantage gained since 1931 would not be lost. On June 16, Sprague and Harrison concluded an agreement with the British and French for temporary stabilization of the three currencies, setting the dollar-sterling rate at about $4 per pound, and pledging the United States not to engage in massive inflation of the currency for the duration of the agreement.

The American representatives urged Roosevelt to accept the agreement, Sprague warning that "a failure now would be most disastrous," and Warburg declaring that without stabilization "it would be practically impossible to assume a leading role in attempting [to] bring about a lasting economic peace." But Roosevelt quickly rejected the agreement on June 17, giving two reasons: that the pound must be stabilized at no cheaper than $4.25, and that he could not accept any restraint on his freedom of action to inflate in order to raise domestic prices. Roosevelt ominously concluded that "it is my personal view that far too much importance is being placed on existing and temporary fluctuations." And lest the American delegation take his reasoning as a stimulus to renegotiating the agreement, Roosevelt reminded Hull on June 20: "Remember that far too much influence is attached to exchange stability by banker-influenced cabinets." Upon receiving the presidential veto, the British and French were indignant, and George Harrison quit and returned home in disgust; but the American delegation went ahead and issued its official statement on temporary currency stabilization on June 22. It declared temporary stabilization impermissible, "because the American government feels that its efforts to raise prices are the most important contribution it can make. . ."[29]

With temporary stabilization scuttled, the conference settled down to longer-range discussions, the most important work being centered in the subcommission on "immediate measures of financial reconstruction" of the Monetary and Financial Commission of the conference. The British delegation began by introducing a draft resolution (1) emphasizing the importance of "cheap and plentiful credit" in order to raise the world level of commodity prices and (2) stating that "the central banks of the principal countries should undertake to cooperate with a view to securing these conditions and should announce their intention of pursuing vigorously a policy of cheap and plentiful money by open market operations."[30] The British thus laid stress on coordinated inflation, but said nothing about the sticking point: exchange rate stabilization. The Dutch, the Czechoslovaks, the Japanese, and the Swiss criticized the British advocacy of inflation, and the Italian delegate warned that "to put one's faith in immediate measures for augmenting the volume of money and credit might lead to a speculative boom followed by an even worse slump . . . a hasty and unregulated flood [of credit] would lead to destructive results." And the French delegate stressed that no genuine recovery could occur without a sense of economic and financial security:

> Who would be prepared to lend, with the fear of being repaid in depreciated currency always before his eyes? Who would find the capital for financing vast programs of economic recovery and abolition of unemployment, as long as there is a possibility that economic struggles would be transported to the monetary field? . . . In a word, without stable currency there can be no lasting confidence; while the hoarding of capital continues, there can be no solution.[31]

The American delegation then submitted its own draft proposal, which was similar to the British, ignored currency stability, and advocated close cooperation between all governments and central banks for "the carrying out of a policy of making credit abundantly and readily available to sound enterprise," especially

[29]Pasvolsky, *Current Monetary Issues*, p. 70. Also see Schlesinger, *Coming of the New Deal*, pp. 213–16; Ferrell, *American Diplomacy*, p. 266.

[30]Pasvolsky, *Current Monetary Issues*, pp. 71–72.

[31]Ibid., pp. 72–74.

by open market operations which expanded the money supply. Also government expenditures and deficits should be synchronized between the different nations.

The difference of views between the nations on inflation and prices, however, precluded any agreement in this area at the conference. On the gold question, Great Britain submitted a policy declaration and the United States a draft resolution which looked forward to eventual restoration of the gold standard—but again, nothing was spelled out on exchange rates, or on the crucial question of whether restoration of price inflation should come first. In both the American and British proposals, however, even the eventual gold standard would be considerably more inflationary than it had been in the 1920s: for all domestic gold circulation, whether coin or bullion, would be abolished, and gold used only as a medium for settling international balances of payment; and all gold reserves ratios to currency would be lowered.[32]

As could have been predicted before the conference, there were three sets of views on gold and currency stabilization. The United States, backed only by Sweden, favored cheap money in order to raise domestic prices, with currency stabilization to be deferred until a sufficient price rise had occurred. Whatever international cooperation was envisaged would stress joint inflationary action to raise price levels in some coordinate manner. The United States, moreover, went further even than Sweden in calling for reflating wholesale prices back to 1926 levels. The gold bloc attacked currency and price inflation, pointed to the early postwar experience of severe inflation and currency depreciation, and hence insisted on stabilization of exchanges and the avoidance of depreciation. In the confused middle were the British and the sterling bloc, who wanted price reflation and cheap credit, but also wanted eventual return to the gold standard and temporary stabilization of the key currencies.

As the London Conference foundered on its severe disagreements, the gold bloc countries began to panic. For on the one hand the dollar was falling in the exchange markets, thus making American goods and currency more competitive. And what is more, the general gloom at the conference gave international speculators the idea that in the near future many of these coun-

[32]Ibid., pp. 74–76, 158–60, 163–66.

tries would themselves be forced to go off gold. In consequence, money began to flow out of these countries during June, and Holland and Switzerland lost over 10 percent of their gold reserves during that month alone. In consequence, the gold countries launched a final attempt to draft a compromise resolution. The proposed resolution was a surprisingly mild one. It committed the signatory countries to reestablishing the gold standard and stable exchange rates, but deliberately emphasized that the parity and date for each country to return to gold was strictly up to each individual country. The existing gold standard countries were pledged to remain on gold, which was not difficult since that was their fervent hope. The nongold countries were to reaffirm their ultimate objective to return to gold, to try their best to limit exchange speculation in the meanwhile, and to cooperate with other central banks in these two endeavors. The innocuousness of the proposed declaration comes from the fact that it committed the United States to very little more than its own resolution of over a week earlier to return eventually to the gold standard, coupled with a vague agreement to cooperate in limiting exchange speculation in the major currencies.

The joint declaration was agreed upon by Sprague, Warburg, James M. Cox, head of the Monetary Commission at the conference, and by Raymond Moley, who had taken charge of the delegation as a freewheeling White House advisor. Moley was assistant secretary of state and had been a monetary nationalist. Moley, however, sent the declaration to Roosevelt on June 30, urging the president to accept it, especially since Roosevelt had been willing a few weeks earlier to stabilize at a $4.25 pound while the depreciation of the dollar during June had now brought the market rate up to $4.40. Across the Atlantic, Undersecretary of the Treasury Dean G. Acheson, influential Wall Street financier Bernard M. Baruch, and Lewis W. Douglas also strongly endorsed the London declaration.

Not hearing immediately from the president, Moley frantically wired Roosevelt the next morning that "success even continuance of the conference depends upon United States agreement."[33] Roosevelt cabled his rejection on July 1, declaring that "a suffi-

---

[33]Schlesinger, *Coming of the New Deal,* pp. 218–21; Pasvolsky, *Current Monetary Issues,* pp. 80–82.

cient interval should be allowed the United States to permit . . . a demonstration of the value of price lifting efforts which we have well in hand.'' Roosevelt's rejection of the innocuous agreement was in itself startling enough; but he felt that he had to add insult to injury, to slash away at the London Conference so that no danger might exist of currency stabilization or of the reconstruction of an international monetary order. Hence he sent on July 3 an arrogant and contemptuous public message to the London Conference, the famous "bombshell" message, so named for its impact on the conference.

Roosevelt began by lambasting the idea of temporary currency stabilization, which he termed a "specious fallacy," an "artificial and temporary . . . diversion." Instead, Roosevelt declared that the emphasis must be placed on "the sound internal economic system of a nation." In particular, "old fetishes of so-called international bankers are being replaced by efforts to plan national currencies with the objective of giving to those currencies a continuing purchasing power which . . . a generation hence will have the same purchasing and debt-paying power as the dollar value we hope to attain in the near future. That objective means more to the good of other nations than a fixed ratio for a month or two in terms of the pound or franc." In short, the president was now totally committed to the nationalist Fisher–Committee of the Nation program for paper money, currency inflation and very steep reflation of prices, and then stabilization of the higher international price level. The idea of stable exchange rates and an international monetary order could fade into limbo.[34] The World Economic Conference limped along aimlessly for a few more weeks, but the Roosevelt bombshell message effectively killed the conference, and the hope for a restored international monetary order was dead for a fateful decade. From here on in the 1930s, monetary nationalism, currency blocs, and commercial and financial warfare would be the order of the day.

The French were bitter and the English stricken at the Roosevelt message. The chagrined James P. Warburg promptly resigned as financial adviser to the delegation, and this was to be the beginning of the exit of this highly placed economic adviser from the

[34]The full text of the Roosevelt message can be found in Pasvolsky, *Current Monetary Issues,* pp. 83–84, or Ferrell, *American Diplomacy,* pp. 270–72.

Roosevelt administration. A similar fate was in store for Oliver Sprague and Dean Acheson. As for Raymond Moley, who had been repudiated by the president's action, he tried to restore himself in Roosevelt's graces by a fawning and obviously insincere telegram, only to be ousted from office shortly after his return to the States. Playing an ambivalent role in the entire affair, Bernard Baruch, who was privately in favor of the old gold standard, praised Roosevelt fulsomely for his message: "Until each nation puts its house in order by the same Herculean efforts that you are performing," Baruch wrote the president, "there can be no common denominators by which we can endeavor to solve the problems. ... There seems to be one common ground that all nations can take, and that is the one outlined by you."[35]

Expressions of enthusiastic support for the president's decision came, as might be expected, from Irving Fisher and George F. Warren, who urged Roosevelt to avoid any possible agreement that might limit "our freedom to change the dollar any day." James A. Farley has recorded in his memoirs that Roosevelt was prompted to send his angry message by coming to suspect a plot to influence Moley in favor of stabilization by Thomas W. Lamont, partner of J. P. Morgan and Co., working through Moley's conference aide and White House advisor, Herbert Bayard Swope, who was close to the Morgans and also a longtime confidant of Baruch. This might well account for Roosevelt's bitter reference to the "so-called international bankers." The situation is curious, however, since Swope was firmly on the antistabilizationist side, and Roosevelt's London message was greeted enthusiastically by Russell Leffingwell of Morgans, who apparently took little notice of its attack on international bankers. Leffingwell wrote to the president: "You were very right not to enter into any temporary or permanent arrangements to peg the dollar in relation to sterling or any other currency."[36]

From the date of the torpedoing of the London Economic Conference, monetary nationalism prevailed for the remainder of the 1930s. The United States finally fixed the dollar at $35 an ounce in January 1934, amounting to a two-thirds increase in the gold price

[35]Schlesinger, *Coming of the New Deal,* p. 224. For Baruch's private views, see Margaret Coit, *Mr. Baruch* (Boston: Houghton Mifflin, 1957), pp. 432–34.

[36]Schlesinger, *Coming of the New Deal,* p. 224; Ferrell, *American Diplomacy,* pp. 273 ff.

of the dollar from its original moorings less than a year before, and to a 40 percent devaluation of the dollar. The gold nations continued on gold for two more years, but the greatly devalued dollar now began to attract a flood of gold from the gold countries, and France was finally forced off gold in the fall of 1936, with the other major gold countries—Switzerland, Belgium, and Holland—following shortly thereafter. While the dollar was technically fixed in terms of gold, there was no further gold coin or bullion redemption within the United States. Gold was used only as a method of clearing balances of payments, with only fitful redemption to foreign countries.

The only significant act of international collaboration after 1934 came in the fall of 1936, at about the time France was forced to leave the gold standard. Partly to assist the French, the United States, Great Britain, and France entered into a Tripartite Agreement, beginning on September 25, 1936. The French agreed to throw in the exchange rate sponge, and devalued the franc by between one-fourth and one-third. At this new par, the three governments agreed—*not* to stabilize their currencies—but to iron out day-to-day fluctuations in them, to engage in mutual stabilization of each other's currencies only within each 24-hour period. This was scarcely stabilization, but it did constitute a moderating of fluctuations, as well as politico-monetary collaboration, which began with the three Western countries and soon expanded to include the other former gold nations: Belgium, Holland, and Switzerland. This collaboration continued until the outbreak of World War II.[37]

At least one incident marred the harmony of the Tripartite Agreement. In the fall of 1938, while the United States and Britain were hammering out a trade agreement, the British began pushing the pound below $4.80. At the threat of this cheapening of the pound, U.S. Treasury officials warned Secretary of the Treasury Henry Morgenthau, Jr., that if "sterling drops substantially below $4.80, our foreign and domestic business will be adversely affected." In consequence Morgenthau successfully insisted that the trade agreement with Britain must include a clause that the

[37]On the Tripartite Agreement, see Raymond F. Mikesell, *United States Economic Policy and International Relations* (New York: McGraw-Hill, 1952), pp. 55–59; W. H. Steiner and E. Shapiro, *Money and Banking* (New York: Henry Holt, 1941), pp. 85–87, 91–93; and Anderson, *Economics and the Public Welfare,* pp. 414–20.

agreement would terminate if Britain should allow the pound to fall below $4.80.[38]

Here we may only touch on a fascinating historical problem which has been discussed by revisionist historians of the 1930s: To what extent was the American drive for war against Germany the result of anger and conflict over the fact that, in the 1930s world of economic and monetary nationalism, the Germans, under the guidance of Dr. Hjalmar Schacht, went their way successfully on their own, totally outside of Anglo-American control or of the confinements of what remained of the cherished American Open Door?[39] A brief treatment of this question will serve as a prelude to examining the aim of the war-borne "second New Deal" of reconstructing a new international monetary order, an order that in many ways resembled the lost world of the 1920s.

German economic nationalism in the 1930s was, first of all, conditioned by the horrifying experience that Germany had had with runaway inflation and currency depreciation during the early 1920s, culminating in the monetary collapse of 1923. Though caught with an overvalued par as each European country went off the gold standard, no German government could have politically succeeded in engaging once again in the dreaded act of devaluation. No longer on gold, and unable to devalue the mark, Germany was obliged to engage in strict exchange control. In this economic climate, Dr. Schacht was particularly successful in making bilateral trade agreements with individual countries, agreements which amounted to direct "barter" arrangements that angered the United States and other Western countries in totally bypassing gold and other international banking or financial arrangements.

---

[38]Lloyd C. Gardner, *Economic Aspects of New Deal Diplomacy* (Madison, Wisc.: University of Wisconsin Press, 1964), p. 107.

[39]For revisionist emphasis on this economic basis for the American drive toward war with Germany, see L. Gardner, *New Deal Diplomacy,* pp. 98–108; Lloyd C. Gardner, "The New Deal, New Frontiers, and the Cold War: A Re-examination of American Expansion, 1933–1945," in D. Horowitz, ed., *Corporations and the Cold War* (New York: Monthly Review Press, 1969), pp. 105–41; William Appleman Williams, *The Tragedy of American Diplomacy* (Cleveland, Oh.: World Pub. Co., 1959), pp. 127–47; Robert Freeman Smith, "American Foreign Relations, 1920–1942," in Barton J. Bernstein, ed., *Towards a New Past* (New York: Pantheon Books, 1968), pp. 245–62; Charles Callan Tansill, *Back Door to War* (Chicago: Henry Regnery, 1952), pp. 441–42.

In the anti-German propaganda of the 1930s, the German barter deals were agreements in which Germany somehow invariably emerged as coercive victor and exploiter of the other country involved, even though they were mutually agreed upon and therefore presumably mutually beneficial exchanges.[40] Actually, there was nothing either diabolic or unilaterally exploitive about the barter deals. Part of the essence of the barter arrangements has been neglected by historians—the deliberate overvaluation of the exchange rates of *both* currencies involved in the deals. The German mark we have seen was deliberately overvalued as the alternative to the specter of currency depreciation; the situation of the other currencies was a bit more complex. Thus, in the barter agreements between Germany and the various Balkan countries (especially Rumania, Hungary, Bulgaria, and Yugoslavia), in which the Balkans exchanged agricultural products for German manufactured goods, the Balkan currencies were also fixed at an artificially overvalued rate vis-à-vis gold and the currencies of Britain and the other Western countries. This meant that Germany agreed to pay higher than world market rates for Balkan agricultural pro ducts while the latter paid higher rates for German manufactured products. For the Balkan countries, the point of all this was to force Balkan consumers of manufactured goods to subsidize their own peasants and agriculturists. The external consequence was that Germany was able to freeze out Britain and other Western countries from buying Balkan food and raw materials; and since the British could not compete in paying for Balkan produce, the Balkan countries, in the bilateral world of the 1930s, did not have sufficient pounds or dollars to buy manufactured goods from the West. Thus, Britain and the West were deprived of raw materials and markets for their manufactures by the astute policies of Hjalmar Schacht and the mutually agreeable barter agreements between Germany and the Balkan and other, including Latin American, countries.[41] May not

[40]Thus, see Douglas Miller, *You Can't Do Business With Hitler* (Boston, 1941), esp. pp. 73–77; and Michael A. Heilperin, *The Trade of Nations* (New York: Alfred Knopf, 1947), pp. 114–17. Miller was commercial attaché at the U.S. Embassy in Berlin throughout the 1930s.

[41]For an explanation of the workings of the German barter agreements, see Ludwig von Mises, *Human Action* (New Haven: Yale University Press, 1949), pp. 796–99. Also on the agreements, see Hjalmar Schacht, *Confessions of "The Old Wizard"* (Boston: Houghton Mifflin, 1956), pp. 302–5.

Western anger at successful German competition through bilateral agreements, and Western desire to liquidate such competition, have been an important factor in the Western drive for war against Germany?

Lloyd Gardner has demonstrated the early hostility of the United States toward German economic controls and barter arrangements, its attempts to pressure Germany to shift to a multilateral, "Open Door" system for American products, and the repeated American rebuffs to German proposals for bilateral exchanges between the two countries. As early as June 26, 1933, the influential American consul-general at Berlin, George Messersmith, was warning that such continued policies would make "Germany a danger to world peace for years to come."[42] In pursuing this aggressive policy, President Roosevelt overrode AAA chief George Peek, who favored accepting bilateral deals with Germany and, perhaps not coincidentally, was to be an ardent "isolationist" in the late 1930s. Instead, Roosevelt followed the policy of the leading interventionist and spokesman for an "Open Door" to American products, Secretary of State Cordell Hull, as well as his Assistant Secretary Francis B. Sayre, son-in-law of Woodrow Wilson. By 1935 American officials were calling Germany an "aggressor" because of its successful bilateral trade competition, and Japan was similarly castigated for much the same reasons. By late 1938 J. Pierrepont Moffat, head of the Western European division of the State Department, was complaining that German control of Central and Eastern Europe would mean "a still further extension of the area under a closed economy." And, more specifically, in May 1940 Assistant Secretary of State Breckenridge Long warned that a German-dominated Europe would mean that "every commercial order will be routed to Berlin and filled under its orders somewhere in Europe rather than in the United States,"[43] And shortly before American entry into the war, John M. McCloy, later to be U.S. High Commissioner of occupied Germany, was to write in a draft for a speech by Secretary of War Henry Stimson: "With German control of the buyers of Europe and her practice of governmental

---

[42]L. Gardner, *New Deal Diplomacy,* p. 98.
[43]Smith, "American Foreign Relations," p. 247; L. Gardner, *New Deal Diplomacy,* p. 99.

control of all trade, it would be well within her power as well as the pattern she has thus far displayed, to shut off our trade with Europe, with South America and with the Far East.''[44]

Not only were Hull and the United States ardent in pressing an anti-German policy against its bilateral trade system, but sometimes Secretary Hull had to whip even Britain into line. Thus, in early 1936, Cordell Hull warned the British ambassador that the ''clearing arrangements reached by Britain with Argentina, Germany, Italy and other countries were handicapping the efforts of this Government to carry forward its broad program with the favored-nation policy underlying it.'' The tendency of these British arrangements was to ''drive straight toward bilateral trading'' and they were therefore milestones on the road to war.[45]

One of the United States government's biggest economic worries was the growing competition of Germany and its bilateral trade in Latin America. As early as 1935, Cordell Hull had concluded that Germany was ''straining every tendon to undermine United States trading relations with Latin America.''[46] A great deal of political pressure was used to combat their competition. Thus, in the mid-1930s, the American Chamber of Commerce in Brazil repeatedly pressed the State Department to scuttle the Germany-Brazil barter deal, which the chamber termed the ''greatest single obstacle to free trade in South America.'' Brazil was finally induced to cancel its agreement with Germany in exchange for a sixty-million dollar loan from the United States. America's exporters, grouped in the National Foreign Trade Council, issued resolutions against German trade methods, and pressured the government for stronger action. And in late 1938 President Roosevelt asked Professor James Harvey Rogers, an economist and disciple of Irving Fisher, to make a currency study of all of South America in order to minimize ''German and Italian influence on this side of the Atlantic.''

It is no wonder that German diplomats in Brazil, Chile, and Uruguay reported home that the United States was ''exerting very strong pressure against Germany commercially,'' which included economic, commercial, and political opposition designed to drive

---

[44]L. Gardner, ''New Deal, New Frontiers,'' p. 118.
[45]Tansill, *Back Door to War,* p. 441.
[46]Smith, ''American Foreign Relations,'' p. 247.

Germany out of the Brazilian and other South American markets.[47]

In the spring of 1935, the German ambassador to Washington, desperately anxious to bring an end to American political and economic warfare, asked the United States what Germany could do to end American hostilites. The American answer, which amounted to a demand for unconditional economic surrender, was that Germany abandon its economic policy in favor of America. The American reply "really meant," noted Pierrepont Moffat, "a fundamental acceptance by Germany of our trade philosophy, and a thorough-going partnership with us along the road of equality of treatment and the reduction of trade barriers." The United States further indicated that it was interested that Germany accept, not so much the *principle* of the most-favored nation clause in all international trade, but specifically for *American* exports.[48]

When war broke out in September 1939, Bernard Baruch's reaction was to tell President Roosevelt that "if we keep our prices down there is no reason why we shouldn't get the customers of the belligerent nations that they have had to drop because of the war. And in that event," Baruch exulted, "Germany's barter system will be destroyed."[49] But particularly significant is the retrospective comment made by Secretary Hull. ". . . war did not break out between the United States and any country with which we had been able to negotiate a trade agreement. It is also a fact that, with very few exceptions, the countries with which we signed trade agreements joined together in resisting the Axis. The political lineup follows the economic lineup."[50] Considering that Secretary

---

[47]L. Gardner, *New Deal Diplomacy,* pp. 59–60.

[48]Ibid., p. 103. It might be noted that in the spring of 1936, Secretary Hull refused to settle for a bilateral deal to sell Germany a large store of American cotton; Hull denounced the idea as "blackmail." The predictable result was that in the next couple of years the sources of raw cotton imported into Germany shifted sharply from the United States to Brazil and Egypt, which had been willing to make barter sales of cotton. Ibid., p. 104; Arthur Schweitzer, *Big Business in the Third Reich* (Bloomington, Ind.: Indiana University Press, 1964), p. 316.

[49]Francis Neilson, *The Tragedy of Europe* (Appleton, Wisc.: C. C. Nelson Publishing Co., 1946), V, p. 289. For a brief but illuminating study of German-American trade and currency hostility in the 1930s leading to World War II, see Thomas H. Etzold, *Why America Fought Germany in World War II* (St. Louis: Forums in History, Forum Press, 1973).

[50]Cordell Hull, *Memoirs* (New York, 1948), I, p. 81.

Hull was a leading maker of American foreign policy throughout the 1930s and through World War II, it is certainly a possibility that his remarks should be taken, not as a quaint testimony to Hull's idée fixe on reciprocal trade, but as a positive causal statement of the thrust of American foreign policy. Read in that light, Hull's remark becomes a significant admission rather than a flight of speculative fancy. Reinforcing this interpretation would be a similar reading of the testimony before the House of Representatives in 1945 of top Treasury aide Harry Dexter White, defending the Bretton Woods agreements. White declared: "I think it [a Bretton Woods system] would very definitely have made a considerable contribution to checking the war and possibly might have prevented it. A great many of the devices which Germany and Japan utilized would have been illegal in the international sphere, had these countries been participating members. ..."[51] Is White saying that the Allies deliberately made war upon the Axis because of these bilateral, exchange control, and other competitive devices, which a Bretton Woods—or for that matter a 1920s—system would have precluded?

We may take as our final testimony to the possible economic causes of World War II, the assertion by the influential *Times* of London, well after the start of the war, that "One of the fundamental causes of this war has been the unrelaxing efforts of Germany since 1918 to secure wide enough foreign markets to straighten her finances at the very time when all her competitors were forced by their own debts to adopt exactly the same course. Continuous friction was inevitable."[52]

The Second New Deal: The Dollar Triumphant

Whether and to what extent German economic nationalism was a cause for the American drive toward war, one point is certain: that, even before official American entry into the war, one of America's principal war aims was to reconstruct an international monetary order. A corollary aim was to replace economic nationalism and bilateralism by the Hullian kind of multilateral trading

[51]Richard N. Gardner, *Sterling-Dollar Diplomacy* (Oxford: Clarendon Press, 1956), p. 141.
[52]The *Times* (London), October 11, 1940. Quoted in Neilson, V, p. 286.

and "Open Door" for American goods. But the most insistent drive, and the particularly successful one, was to reconstruct an international monetary system. The system in view was to resemble the gold exchange system of the 1920s quite closely. Once again, all the major world's currencies were to abandon fluctuating and nationally determined exchange rates on behalf of fixed parities with other currencies and of all of them with gold. Once again, there was to be no full-fledged or internal gold standard for any of these nations; while in theory all currencies were to be fixed in terms of one key currency, which would form a "gold exchange" standard on which other nations could pyramid their own supply of domestic money. But there were two crucial differences from the 1920s. One was that while the key currency was to be the only currency redeemable in gold, there was to be no further embarrassing possibility of internal redemption in gold; gold was only to be a method of international payment between central banks, and never again an actual money held by the public. In this way, the key currency—and the rest of the world in response— could expand and inflate much further than in the 1920s, freed as they were from the check of domestic redemption. But the second difference was more politically far-reaching: for instead of two joint-partner key currencies, the pound and the dollar, with the dollar as workhorse junior subaltern, the *only* key currency was now to be the dollar, which was to be fixed at $35 to the gold ounce. The pound had had it; and just as the United States was to use the Second World War to replace British imperialism with its own far-flung empire; so in the monetary sphere, the United States was now to move in and take over, with the pound no less subordinate than all the other major currencies. It was truly a triumphant "dollar imperialism" to parallel the imperial American thrust in the political sphere. As Secretary of the Treasury Henry Morgenthau, Jr., was later to express it, the critical and eminently successful objective was "to move the financial center of the world" from London to the United States Treasury.[53] And all this was eminently in keeping with the prophetic vision of Cordell Hull, the man who, in the words of Gabriel Kolko, had "the basic responsibility for American political and economic planning for the peace." For Hull had urged upon Congress as far back as

[53]R. Gardner, *Sterling-Dollar Diplomacy*, p. 76.

1932, that America "gird itself, yield to the law of manifest destiny, and go forward as the supreme world factor economically and morally."[54]

World War II was the occasion for a new coalition to form behind the New Deal, a coalition which reintegrated many conservative "internationalist" financial interests who had been thrown into opposition by the domestic statism or economic nationalism of the earlier New Deal. This reintegration of the entire conservative financial community was particularly true in the field of international economic and monetary policy. Here, Dr. Leo Pasvolsky, a conservative economist who had broken with the New Deal on the scuttling of the London Economic Conference, returned to a crucial role as Secretary Hull's special advisor on postwar planning. Dean Acheson, also disaffected by the radical monetary measures of 1933–34, was now back as assistant secretary of state for economic affairs. And when the ailing Cordell Hull retired in late 1944, he was replaced by Edward Stettinius, son of a Morgan partner and himself former president of Morgan-oriented U.S. Steel. Stettinius chose as his assistant secretary for economic affairs the man who quickly became the key official for postwar international economic planning, William L. Clayton, a former leader of the anti–New Deal Liberty League and chairman and major partner of Anderson, Clayton & Co., the world's largest cotton export firm. Clayton's major focus in postwar planning was to promote and encourage American exports—with cotton, not unnaturally, never out of the forefront of his concerns.[55]

Even before American entry into the war, U.S. economic war aims were well defined and rather brutally simple: They hinged on a determined assault upon the 1930s system of economic and monetary nationalism, so as to promote American exports, investments, and financial dealings overseas, in short, the "Open Door" for American commerce. In the sphere of commercial policy this took the form of pressure for reduction of tariffs on

[54]Smith, "American Foreign Relations," p. 252; Gabriel Kolko, *The Politics of War: The World and United States Foreign Policy, 1943–45* (New York: Random House, 1968), pp. 243–44.

[55]Kolko, *Politics of War,* pp. 264, 485 ff.; Lloyd C. Gardner, *Architects of Illusion: Men and Ideas in American Foreign Policy, 1941–1949* (Chicago: Quadrangle Books, 1970), pp. 113–38.

American products, and the elimination of quantitative import restrictions on those products. In the allied sphere of monetary policy, it meant the breakup of powerful nationalistic currency blocs, and the restoration of an international monetary order based on the dollar, in which currencies would be convertible into each other at predictable and fixed parities and there would be a minimum of national exchange controls over the purchase and use of foreign currencies.

And even as the United States was prepared to enter the war to save its ally, Great Britain, it was preparing to bludgeon the British at a time of great peril into abandoning their sterling bloc, which they had organized effectively since the Ottawa Agreements of 1932. World War II would presumably deal effectively with the German bilateral trade and currency menace; but what about the problem of Great Britain?

John Maynard Keynes had long led those British economists who had urged a policy of all-out economic and monetary nationalism on behalf of inflation and full employment. He had gone so far as to hail Roosevelt's torpedoing of the London Economic Conference because the path was then cleared for economic nationalism. Keynes's visit to Washington on behalf of the British government in the summer of 1941 now spread gloom about the British determination to continue their bilateral economic policies after the war. High State Department official J. Pierrepont Moffat despaired that "the future is clouding up rapidly and that despite the war the Hitlerian commercial policy will probably be adopted by Great Britain."[56]

The United States responded by putting the pressure on Great Britain at the Atlantic Conference in August 1941. Under Secretary of State Sumner Welles insisted that the British agree to remove discrimination against American exports, and abolish their policies of autarchy, exchange controls, and Imperial Preference blocs.[57] Prime Minister Churchill tartly refused, but the United States was scarcely prepared to abandon its crucial aim of breaking down the sterling bloc. As President Roosevelt privately told his son Elliott at the Atlantic Conference:

[56]L. Gardner, "New Deal, New Frontiers," p. 120.
[57]R. Gardner, *Sterling-Dollar Diplomacy,* pp. 42 ff.; L. Gardner, *New Deal Diplomacy,* pp. 275–80.

It's something that's not generally known, but British bankers and German bankers have had world trade pretty well sewn up in their pockets for a long time.... Well, now, that's not so good for American trade, is it?... If in the past German and British economic interests have operated to exclude us from world trade, kept our merchant shipping closed down, closed us out of this or that market, and now Germany and Britain are at war, what should we do?[58]

The signing of Lend-Lease agreements was the ideal time for wringing concessions from the British, but Britain consented to sign the agreement's article VII, which merely involved a vague commitment to the elimination of discriminatory treatment in international trade, only after intense pressure by the United States. The agreement was signed at the end of February 1942, and in return the State Department pledged to the British that the United States would pursue a policy of economic expansion and full employment after the war. Even under these conditions, however, Britain soon maintained that the Lend-Lease Agreement committed it to virtually nothing. To Cordell Hull, however, the agreement on article VII was decisive and constituted "a long step toward the fulfillment, after the war, of the economic principles for which I had been fighting for half a century." The United States also insisted that other nations receiving Lend-Lease sign a virtually identical commitment to multilateralism after the war. In his first major public address in nearly a year, Hull, in July 1942, could now look forward confidently that "leadership toward a new system of international relationships in trade and other economic affairs will devolve very largely upon the United States because of our great economic strength. We should assume this leadership, and the responsibility that goes with it, primarily for reasons of pure national self-interest."[59]

In the postwar planning for economic affairs, the State Department was in charge of commercial and trade policies, while the Treasury conducted the planning in the areas of money and finance. In charge of postwar international financial planning for the Treasury was the economist Harry Dexter White. In early 1942, White presented his first plan which was to be one of the two major foundations of the postwar monetary system. White's

[58]Smith, "American Foreign Relations," p. 252; Kolko, *Politics of War,* pp. 248–49.

[59]Kolko, *Politics of War,* pp. 249–51.

proposal was of course within the framework of American post-war economic objectives. The countries of the world were to join a stabilization fund, totalling $5 billion, which would lend funds at short term to deficit countries to iron out temporary balance-of-payments difficulties. But in return for this provision of greater liquidity and short-term aid to deficit countries, exchange rates of currencies were to be fixed, in relation to the dollar and hence to gold, with the gold price to be set at $35 an ounce, and exchange controls were to be abandoned by the various nations.

While the White Plan envisioned a substantial amount of infla-tion to provide greater currency liquidity, the British responded with a Keynes Plan that was far more inflationary. By this time, Lord Keynes had abandoned economic and monetary nationalism for Britain under severe American pressure, and his aim was to salvage as much domestic inflation and cheap money for Britain as he could possibly induce America to accept. The Keynes Plan envisioned an International Clearing Union, which, in return for agreeing to stable exchange rates between currencies and the abandonment of exchange control, provided a huge loan fund to its members of $26 billion. The Keynes Plan, moreover, provided for a new international monetary unit, the "bancor," which could be issued by the ICU in such large amounts as to provide almost unchecked room for inflation, even in a country with a large deficit in its balance of payments. The nations would consult with each other about correcting balance of payments disequili-bria, through altering their exchange rates. The Keynes Plan, fur-thermore, provided automatic access to the fund of liquidity, with none of the embarrassing requirements, as included in the White Plan, for deficit countries to cease creating deficits by inflating their currency. Whereas the White Plan authorized the Stabiliza-tion Fund to require deficit countries to cease inflating in return for fund loans, the Keynes Plan envisioned that inflation would proceed unchecked, with all the burden of necessary adjustments to be placed on the hard-money, creditor countries, who would be expected to inflate faster themselves, in order not to gain currency from the deficit nations.

The White Plan was stringently attacked by the conservative nationalists and inflationists in Britain, particularly G. R. Booth-by, Lord Beaverbrook, the London *Times* and the *Economist*. The Keynes Plan was attacked by conservatives in the United

States, as was even the White Plan for interfering with market forces and for automatic extension of credit to deficit countries. Critical of the White Plan were the Guaranty Survey of the Guaranty Trust Co., and the American Bankers Association; furthermore, the New York *Times* and New York *Herald Tribune* called for return to the classical gold standard and attacked the large measure of governmental financial planning envisioned by both the Keynes and White proposals.[60]

After negotiating during 1943 and until the spring of 1944, the United States and Britain hammered out a compromise of the White and Keynes Plans in April, 1944. The compromise was adopted by a world economic conference in July at Bretton Woods, New Hampshire; it was Bretton Woods that was to provide the monetary framework for the postwar world.[61]

The compromise established an International Monetary Fund as the stabilization mechanism; its total funds were fixed at $8.8 billion, far closer to the White than the Keynes prescriptions. Its balance of IMF international control as against domestic autonomy lay between the White and Keynes plans, leaving the whole problem highly fuzzy. On the one hand, national access to the fund was *not* to be automatic; but on the other, the fund could no longer require corrective domestic economic policies of its members. On the question of exchange rates, the Americans yielded to the British insistence on allowing room for domestic inflation even at the expense of stable exchange rates. The compromise provided that each country could be free to make a 10 percent change in its exchange rate, and that larger changes could be made to correct "fundamental disequilibria"; in short, that a chronically deficit country could devalue its currency rather than check its own inflation. Furthermore, the United States yielded again in allowing creditor countries to suffer by permitting deficit countries to impose exchange controls on "scarce currencies." This meant in effect that the major European countries, whose currencies would be fixed at existing highly overvalued rates in relation to the dollar, would thus be permitted to enter the IMF with

[60]R. Gardner, *Sterling-Dollar Diplomacy,* pp. 71 ff., 95–99.

[61]We do not deal here with the other institution established at Bretton Woods, the International Bank for Reconstruction and Development, which, in contrast to the International Monetary Fund, comes under commercial and financial, rather than monetary, policy.

chronically overvalued currencies and then impose exchange controls on "scarce," undervalued dollars. But despite these extensive concessions, there was no "bancor"; the dollar, fixed at $35 per gold ounce was now to be firmly established as the key currency base of a new world monetary order. Besides, for the dollar to be undervalued and other major currencies to be overvalued greatly spurs American exports, which was one of the basic aims of the entire operation. U.S. Ambassador to Britain John G. Winant recorded the perceptive hostility to the Bretton Woods Agreement by the majority of the directors of the Bank of England; for these men saw "that if the plan is adopted financial control will leave London and sterling exchange will be replaced by dollar exchange."[62]

The proposed International Monetary Fund ran into a storm of conservative opposition in the United States, from the opposite pole of the hostility of the British nationalists. The American attack on the IMF was essentially launched by two major groups: conservative Eastern bankers and midwestern isolationists. Among the bankers, the American Bankers' Association attacked the unsound and inflationary policy of allowing debtor countries to control access to international funds; and W. Randolph Burgess, president of the ABA, denounced the provision for debtor rationing of "scarce currencies" as an "abomination." The New York *Times* urged rejection of the IMF, and proposed making loans to Britain in exchange for the abolition of exchange controls and quantitative restrictions on imports. Another banker group came up with a "key currency" proposal as a substitute for Bretton Woods. This key currency plan was proposed by economist John H. Williams, vice-president of the Federal Reserve Bank of New York, and endorsed by Leon Fraser, president of the First National Bank of N.Y., and by Winthrop W. Aldrich, head of the Chase National Bank. It envisioned a bilateral pound-dollar stabilization, fueled by a large transitional American loan or even grant to Great Britain. Thus, the key currency people were ready to abandon temporarily not only the classical gold standard but even an international monetary order, and to stay temporarily in a

[62]Winant to Hull, April 12, 1944. In R. Gardner, *Sterling-Dollar Diplomacy,* p. 123. Also see pages 110–21.

modified version of the world of the 1930s.[63]

The midwestern isolationist critics of the IMF were led by Senator Robert A. Taft (R., Ohio), who charged that, while the bulk of the valuable hard-money placed in the fund would be American dollars, the dollars would be subject to international control by the fund authorities, and therefore by the debtor countries. The debtor countries could then still continue exchange controls and sterling bloc practices. Here Taft failed to realize that formal and informal structures in the Bretton Woods design would insure effective United States control of both the IMF and the International Bank.[64]

The administration countered the critics of Bretton Woods with a massive propaganda campaign, which was able to drive the agreement through Congress by mid-July 1945. It emphasized that the U.S. government would have effective control, at least of its own representatives in the fund. It played up—in what proved to be gross exaggeration—the favorable aspects of the various ambiguous provisions: insisting that debtor access to the fund would not be automatic, that exchange controls would be removed, and that exchange rates would be stabilized. It pushed heavily the vague idea that the fund was crucial to postwar international cooperation to keep the peace. Particularly interesting was the argument of Will Clayton and others that Bretton Woods would facilitate the general commercial policy of eliminating trade discrimination and barriers against American exports. This argument was put particularly baldly by Secretary of the Treasury Morgenthau in a speech to Detroit industrialists. Morgenthau promised that the Bretton Woods agreement would lead to a world trade freed from exchange controls and depreciated currencies, and that this would greatly increase the exports of American automobiles. Since the fund would begin operations the following year by accepting the existing grossly overvalued currency parities that most

[63] An elaboration of the banker-oriented criticisms of the fund may be found in Anderson, *Economics and the Public Welfare,* pp. 578–89.

[64] Henry W. Berger, "Senator Robert A. Taft Dissents from Military Escalation," in Thomas G. Paterson, ed., *Cold War Critics: Alternatives to American Foreign Policy in the Truman Years* (Chicago: Quadrangle Books, 1971), pp. 174–75, 198. Taft also strongly opposed the government's guaranteeing of private foreign investments, such as were involved in the International Bank program. Ibid. Also see Kolko, *Politics of War,* pp. 256–57; L. Gardner, *New Deal Diplomacy,* p. 287; and Mikesell, *United States Economic Policy,* pp. 199 ff.

of the nations insisted upon, this meant that Morgenthau might have known whereof he spoke. For if other currencies are overvalued and the dollar undervalued, American exports are indeed encouraged and subsidized.[65]

It is perhaps understandable, then, that not only the major farm, labor, and New Deal liberal organizations pushed for Bretton Woods, but also that the large majority of industrial and financial interests also approved the agreements and urged its passage in Congress. American approval in mid-1945 was followed, after lengthy soul-searching, by the approval of Great Britain at the end of the year. By the end of its existence, therefore, the second New Deal had established the triumphant dollar as the base of a new international monetary order.[66] The dollar had displaced the pound, and within a general political framework in which the American Empire had replaced the British. Looking forward perceptively to the postwar world in January 1945, Lamar Fleming, Jr., president of Anderson, Clayton & Co., wrote to his longtime colleague Will Clayton that the "British empire and British international influence is a myth already." The United States would soon become the British protector against the emerging Russian landmass, prophesied Fleming, and this will mean "the absorption into [the] American empire of the parts of the British Empire which we will be willing to accept."[67] As the New Deal came to a close, the triumphant United States stood ready to reap its fruits on a worldwide scale.

Epilogue

The Bretton Woods agreement established the framework for the international monetary system down to the early 1970s. A new and more restricted international dollar-gold exchange standard had replaced the collapsed dollar-pound-gold exchange standard of the 1920s. During the early postwar years, the system worked

[65]R. Gardner, *Sterling-Dollar Diplomacy,* pp. 136–37; Mikesell, *United States Economic Policy,* pp. 134 ff.

[66]On the American debate over Bretton Woods, see R. Gardner, *Sterling-Dollar Diplomacy,* pp. 129–43; on Bretton Woods, also see Mikesell, *United States Economic Policy,* pp. 129–35, 138 ff., 142 ff., 149–52, 155–58, 163–70.

[67]Kolko, *Politics of War,* p. 294.

quite successfully within its own terms, and the American banking community completely abandoned its opposition.[68] With the European currencies inflated and overvalued, and European economies exhausted, the undervalued dollar was the strongest and "hardest" of world currencies, a world "dollar shortage" prevailed, and the dollar could base itself upon the vast stock of gold in the United States, much of which had fled from war and devastation abroad. But in the early 1950s, the world economic balance began slowly but emphatically to change. For while the United States, influenced by Keynesian economics, proceeded blithely to inflate the dollar, seemingly relieved of the limits imposed by the classical gold standard, several European countries began to move in the opposite direction. Under the revived influence of conservative, free-market and hard-money oriented economists in such countries as West Germany, France, Italy, and Switzerland, these newly recovered countries began to achieve prosperity with far less inflated currencies. Hence these currencies became ever stronger and "harder" while the dollar became softer and increasingly inflated.[69]

The continuing inflation of the dollar began to have two important consequences: (1) that the dollar was increasingly overvalued in relation to gold; and (2) that the dollar was also increasingly overvalued in relation to the West German mark, the French and Swiss francs, the Japanese yen, and other hard-money currencies. The result was a chronic and continuing deficit in the American balance of payments, beginning in the early 1950s and persisting ever since. The consequence of the chronic deficit was a continuing outflow of gold abroad and a heavy piling up of dollar claims in the central banks of the hard money countries. Since 1960 the foreign short-term claims to American gold have therefore become increasingly greater than the U.S. gold supply. In short, just as inflation in England and the United States during the 1920s

[68]The removal of such classical progold standard economists as Henry Hazlitt from his post as editorial writer for the *New York Times,* and of Dr. B. M. Anderson from the Chase National Bank, coincided with the accommodation of the financial community to the new system.

[69]We might mention the influence of such economists as Ludwig Erhard, Alfred Müller-Armack, and Wilhelm Ropke in Germany, President Luigi Einaudi in Italy, and Jacques Rueff in France, who had played a similar hard-money role in the 1920s and early 1930s.

led finally to the breakdown of the international monetary order, so has inflation in the postwar key country, the United States, led to increasing strains and fissures in the triumphant dollar order of the post World War II world. It has become increasingly evident that an ever more inflated and overvalued dollar cannot continue as the permanently secure base of the world monetary system, and therefore that this ever more strained and insecure system cannot long continue in anything like its present form.

In fact, the postwar system has already been changed considerably, in an ultimately futile attempt to preserve its basic features. In the spring of 1968, a severe monetary run on the dollar by Europeans redeeming dollar claims led to two major changes. One was the partial abandonment of the fixed $35 per ounce gold price. Instead, a two-price, or "two-tier," gold price system was established. The dollar and gold were allowed to find their own level in the free gold markets of the world, with the United States no longer standing ready to support the dollar in the gold market at $35 an ounce. On the other hand, $35 still continued as the supposedly eternally fixed price for the world central banks, who were pledged not to sell gold in the world market. Keynesian economists were convinced that with the dollar and gold severed on the world market, the price of gold would then fall in the freely fluctuating market. The reverse, however, has occurred, since the world market continued to have more faith in the soundness and the relative hardness of gold than in the increasingly inflated dollar.

The second change was the creation of Special Drawing Rights, a new form of "paper gold," of newly created paper which can supplement gold as an international currency reserve behind each currency. While this indeed put more backing behind the dollar, the quantity of SDR's has been too limited to make an appreciable difference to a world economy that trusts the dollar less with each passing year.

These two minor repairs, however, failed to change the fundamental overvaluation of the ever more inflated dollar. In the spring of 1971, a new monetary crisis finally led to a massive revaluation of the hard currencies. If the United States stubbornly refused to lose face by raising the price of gold or by otherwise devaluing the dollar down to its genuine value in the world market, then the harder currencies, such as West Germany, Switzerland,

and the Netherlands, found themselves reluctantly forced to raise the value of their currencies. Their alternative—a massive calling upon the United States to redeem in gold and thereby the smashing of the façade of dollar redemption in gold—was too much of a political break with the United States for these nations to contemplate. For the United States, to preserve the façade of gold redemption at $35, had been using intense political pressure on its creditors to retain their dollar balances and *not* to redeem them in gold. By the late 1960s, General de Gaulle, under the influence of classical gold-standard advocate Jacques Rueff, was apparently preparing to make just such a challenge—to break the dollar standard as a move toward restoring the classical gold standard in France and much of the rest of Europe. But the French domestic troubles in the spring of 1968 ended that dream at least temporarily, as France was forced to inflate the franc for a time in order to pay the overall wage increase it had agreed upon under the threat of the general strike.

Despite these hasty repairs, it is becoming increasingly evident that they are makeshift stopgaps, and that a series of more aggravated crises will shake the international monetary order until a fundamental change is made. A hard-money policy in the United States that put an end to inflation and increased the soundness of the dollar might sustain the current system, but this is so politically remote as to be hardly a likely prognosis.

There are several possible monetary systems that might replace the present deteriorating order. The new system desired by the Keynesian economists and by the American government would be a massive extension of "paper gold" to demonetize gold completely and replace it by a new monetary unit (such as the Keynesian "bancor") and a paper currency issued by a new world Reserve Bank. If this were achieved, then the new American-dominated world Reserve Bank would be able to inflate any currencies indefinitely, and allow inflating currencies to pay for any and all deficits ad infinitum. While such a scheme, embodied in the Triffin Plan, the Bernstein Plan, and others, is now the American dream, it has met determined opposition by the hard-money countries, and it remains doubtful that the United States will be able to force these countries to go along with the plan.

The other logical alternative is the Rueff Plan, of returning to the classical gold standard after a massive increase in the world price of gold. But this too is unlikely, especially over powerful American opposition. Barring acceptance of a new world currency, the Americans would be content to keep inflating and simply force the hard-money countries to keep appreciating their exchange rates, but again it is doubtful that German, French, Swiss, and other exporters will be content to keep crippling themselves in order to subsidize dollar inflation. Perhaps the most likely prognosis is the formation of a new hard-money European currency bloc, which might eventually be strong enough to challenge the dollar, politically as well as economically. In that case, the dollar standard will probably fall apart, and we may see a return to the currency blocs of the 1930s, with the European bloc this time on a harder and quasi-gold basis. It is at least possible that the future will see gold and the hard European currencies at last dethrone the triumphant but increasingly uneasy dollar.

RECOMMENDED READING

Anderson, Benjamin. *Economics and the Public Welfare: Financial and Economic History of the U.S., 1914–1946.* New York: Van Nostrand, 1949.

———.*The Great Depression.* New York: Macmillan, 1934.

———.*The Value of Money.* New York: Macmillan, 1926.

Baxter, W. T. "The Accountant's Contribution to the Trade Cycle." *Economica,* May 1955, pp. 99–112.

Bresciani-Turroni, Costantino. *The Economics of Inflation: A Study of Currency Depreciation in Post-War Germany.* New York: Kelley, 1976.

Brough, William. *Open Mints and Free Banking.* New York: Putnam, 1894.

Carroll, Charles H. *The Organization of Debt into Currency, and Other Essays.* Princeton, N.J.: Van Nostrand, 1962.

De Roover, Raymond. *Business, Banking, and Economic Thought in Late Medieval and Early Modern Europe.* Chicago: University of Chicago Press, 1974.

Dewey, David R. *Financial History of the United States.* New York: Kelley, 1969.

Farrer, Thomas H. *Studies in Currency, 1898.* New York: Kelley, 1968.

Fetter, Frank A. "Some Neglected Aspects of Gresham's Law." *Quarterly Journal of Economics* 46 (1931–32): 480–95.

Garrett, Garet. *A Bubble That Broke the World.* Boston: Little, Brown, 1932.

Gouge, William M. *A Short History of Paper Money and Banking in the United States.* New York: Kelley, 1968.

Groseclose, Elgin. *Fifty Years of Managed Money: The Story of the Federal Reserve.* New York: Books, Inc., 1966.

———. *Money and Man: A Survey of Monetary Experience.* Norman: University of Oklahoma Press, 1976.

Guttman, Nathan, and Meehan, Patricia. *The Great Inflation: Germany, 1919–1923.* New York: Saxon House, 1975.

Haberler, Gottfried. *Prosperity and Depression: A Theoretical Analysis of Cyclical Movements.* 4th ed., pp. 5–84. Cambridge: Harvard University Press, 1958.

Haberler, G.; Hayek, F. A.; Rothbard, M. N.; and Mises, L. von. *Austrian Theory of the Trade Cycle, and Other Essays.* New York: Center for Libertarian Studies, 1978.

Hawtrey, Ralph G. *The Art of Central Banking.* Clifton, N.J.: Kelley, 1965.

———. *A Century of Bank Rate.* Clifton, N.J.: Kelley, 1965.

Hayek, Friedrich A. *Choice in Currency: A Way to Stop Inflation.* London: Institute of Economic Affairs, 1977.

———. *The Denationalisation of Money.* London: Institute of Economic Affairs, 1976.

———. *Monetary Nationalism and International Stability.* New York: Kelley, 1971.

———. *Monetary Theory and the Trade Cycle.* New York: Kelley, 1975.

———. *New Studies in Philosophy, Politics, Economics, and the History of Ideas,* pp. 165–78, 191–231. Chicago: University of Chicago Press, 1978.

———. *Prices and Production.* New York: Kelley, 1967.

———. *Profits, Interest and Investment, and Other Essays on the Theory of Industrial Fluctuations.* New York: Kelley, 1975.

———. *A Tiger by the Tail: The Keynesian Legacy of Inflation.* San Francisco: Cato Institute, 1979.

Hazlitt, Henry. *The Failure of the "New Economics."* New Rochelle, N.Y.: Arlington House, 1959.

———. *What You Should Know about Inflation.* New York: Funk & Wagnalls, 1968.

————., ed. *The Critics of Keynesian Economics*. New Rochelle, N.Y.: Arlington House, 1977.

Hutt, William H. *The Theory of Idle Resources*. Indianapolis: Liberty Press, 1977.

Jevons, William S. *Money and the Mechanism of Exchange*. London: Kegan Paul, 1905.

Kirzner, Israel M. *The Economic Point of View: An Essay in the History of Economic Thought*, pp. 91–107. Kansas City: Sheed & Ward, 1976.

————. *Perception, Opportunity, and Profit*. Chicago: University of Chicago Press, 1979.

Lachmann, Ludwig M. *Macroeconomic Thinking and the Market Economy*. Menlo Park, Calif.: Institute for Humane Studies, 1978.

Law, John. *Money and Trade Considered*. Clifton, N.J.: Kelley, 1966.

Lindahl, Erik R. *Studies in the Theory of Money and Capital*. New York: Kelley, 1970.

Lutz, Friedrich A. "Essential Properties of a Medium of Exchange." In *Roads to Freedom: Essays in Honour of Friedrich A. Hayek*, edited by E. Streissler, pp. 105–16. London: Routledge & Kegan Paul, 1969.

Machlup, Fritz. *The Stock Market, Credit and Capital Formation*. New York: Macmillan, 1940.

MacManus, T.; Nelson, R.; and Phillips, C. *Banking and the Business Cycle*. New York: Macmillan, 1937.

McGrane, Reginald C. *Foreign Bondholders and American State Debts*. New York: Macmillan, 1935.

Miller, Harry E. *Banking Theories in the United States Before 1860*. New York: Kelley, 1972.

Mises, Ludwig von. *Human Action: A Treatise on Economics*, pp. 398–478, 538–86, 780–803. Chicago: Regnery. 1966.

————. *On the Manipulation of Money and Credit*. Dobbs Ferry, N.Y.: Free Market Books, 1978.

————. *Planning for Freedom and Other Essays and Addresses*. South Holland, Ill.: Libertarian Press, 1962.

————. *Socialism: An Economic and Sociological Analysis*. Translated by J. Kahane. New Haven: Yale University Press, 1951. This edition is translated from the second German edition (1932) of Mises's *Die Gemeinwirtschaft* (1922).

————. *The Theory of Money and Credit.* Irvington-on-Hudson, N.Y.: Foundation for Economic Education, 1971.

O'Driscoll, Gerald P., Jr. *Economics as a Coordination Problem: The Contributions of Friedrich A. Hayek.* Kansas City: Sheed Andrews & McMeel, 1977.

————, and Shenoy, Sudha R. "Inflation, Recession, and Stagflation." In *The Foundations of Modern Austrian Economics,* edited by Edwin G. Dolan, pp. 185–211. Kansas City: Sheed & Ward, 1976.

Palyi, Melchior. *The Inflation Primer.* Chicago: Regnery, 1972.

————. *The Twilight of Gold, 1914–1936: Myths and Realities.* Chicago: Regnery, 1972.

Raquet, Condy. *A Treatise on Currency and Banking.* New York: Kelley, 1967.

Rickenbacker, William F. *Death of the Dollar.* New York: Dell, 1970.

————. *Wooden Nickels, or the Decline and Fall of Silver Coins.* New Rochelle, N.Y.: Arlington House, 1966.

Ringer, Fritz. *The German Inflation of 1923.* New York: Oxford University Press, 1969.

Rist, Charles. *The Triumph of Gold.* Westport, Conn.: Greenwood, 1961.

————. *History of Monetary and Credit Theory.* New York: Kelley, 1966.

Robbins, Lionel. *The Great Depression.* Plainview, N.Y.: Books for Libraries, 1934.

Rothbard, Murray N. *America's Great Depression.* Kansas City: Sheed & Ward, 1975.

————. "Austrian Definitions of the Supply of Money." In *New Directions in Austrian Economics,* edited by Louis M. Spadaro, pp. 143–56. Kansas City: Sheed Andrews & McMeel, 1978.

————. "The Austrian Theory of Money." In *The Foundations of Modern Austrian Economics,* edited by Edwin G. Dolan, pp. 160–84. Kansas City: Sheed & Ward, 1976.

————. *The Case for a 100% Gold Dollar.* Alexandria, Va.: Libertarian Review Press, 1974.

————. *Man, Economy, and State: A Treatise on Economic Principles,* pp. 160–271, 661–759. Los Angeles: Nash, 1970.

————. *The Panic of 1819: Reaction and Policies.* New York: Columbia University Press, 1962.

————. *What Has Government Done to Our Money?* Novato, Calif.: Libertarian Publishers, 1978.

Rueff, Jacques. *The Age of Inflation.* Chicago: Regnery, 1964.

————. *Monetary Sin of the West.* New York: Macmillan, 1972.

Select Committee on the High Price of Gold, House of Commons. *The Paper Pound of 1797–1821.* New York: Kelley, 1969.

Sennholz, Hans, ed. *Gold Is Money.* Westport, Conn.: Greenwood, 1975.

Smith, Vera C. *The Rationale of Central Banking.* London: King, 1936.

Thornton, Henry. *An Inquiry into the Nature and Effects of the Paper Credit of Great Britain.* New York: Kelley, 1965.

Walker, Amasa. *The Science of Wealth.* Boston: Little, Brown, 1867.

Walker, Michael, ed. *The Illusion of Wage and Price Control: Essays on Inflation, Its Cause and Its Cures.* Vancouver, B.C.: Fraser Institute, 1976.

White, Andrew Dickson. *Fiat Money Inflation in France.* San Francisco: The Cato Institute, 1980.

Wicksell, G. Knut. *Interest and Prices: A Study of the Causes Regulating the Value of Money.* Clifton, N.J.: Kelley, 1965.

————. *Lectures on Political Economy.* Clifton, N.J.: Kelley, 1967–68.

Wiegand, G. Carl, ed. *The Menace of Inflation: Its Causes and Consequences.* Old Greenwich, Conn.: Devin-Adair, 1976.

Yeager, Leland B. "Essential Properties of a Medium of Exchange." *Kyklos,* 1968.

ABOUT THE AUTHORS

Garet Garrett (christened Edward Peter Garrett) was born in Pana, Illinois, in 1878. Educated in public schools, by age twenty-five he was a financial writer on the staff of the *New York Sun*. Jobs with the *New York Times*, the *Wall Street Journal*, and the *Evening Post* followed. In 1912 he became editor of the *New York Times Annalist*, and four years later he was named executive editor of the *New York Tribune*.

After three years at the Tribune, Garrett retired to pursue a free-lance career. In the 1920s he wrote seven books and many articles on finance and economic affairs. *The Bubble That Broke the World* appeared in 1932, and Garrett continued writing articles that voiced his concern over New Deal policies. He became editor-in-chief of the *Saturday Evening Post* in 1940, and, in 1944, editor of the magazine *American Affairs*. Notable among his later books are *A Time Is Born* (1944), *The Revolution Was* (1944), and *Rise of Empire* (1951).

Garet Garrett died in 1954.

Murray N. Rothbard received his A.B. in 1945, his A.M. in 1946, and his Ph.D. in economics in 1956—all from Columbia University. He is Professor of Economics at Polytechnic Institute of New York and a Senior Fellow, Cato Institute.

He was an Instructor at City College of New York from 1948 to 1949, a Senior Analyst for the William Volker Fund from 1961 to 1962, and has been an Associate of the University Seminar in the History of Legal and Political Thought at Columbia University since 1964. He is Editor of *The Journal of Libertarian Studies* and Contributing Editor to *Inquiry* magazine and *Libertarian Review*.

Rothbard is the author of *America's Great Depression; Conceived in Liberty* (3 vols.); *For a New Liberty: The Libertarian Manifesto;* and many other works. He has contributed to more than twenty-five books and has written more than forty articles and reviews for scholarly journals.

The Cato Papers

Reprinted by the Cato Institute, the Papers in this series have been selected for their singular contributions to such fields as economics, history, philosophy, and public policy.

Copies of the *Cato Papers* may be ordered from the Publications Department, Cato Institute, 747 Front Street, San Francisco, California 94111.